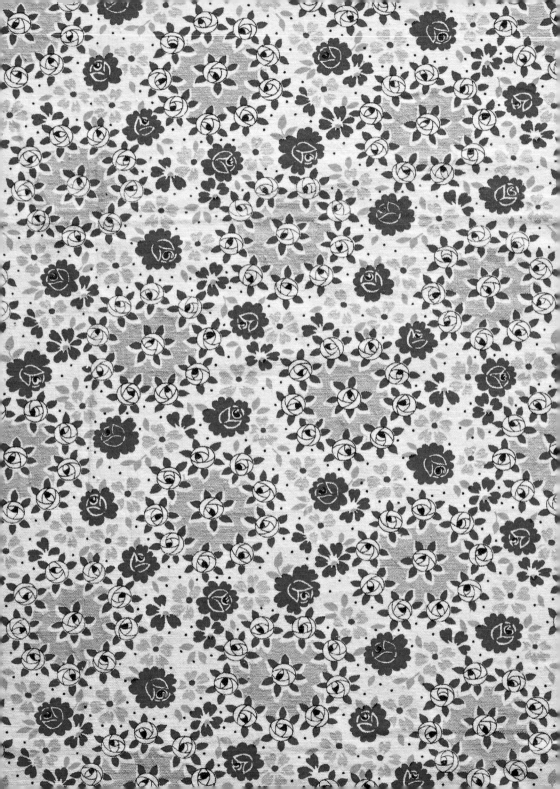

POSH

SANDWICHES

POSH
SANDWICHES

Over 70 recipes,
from Reubens to banh mi

Rosie Reynolds

Photography by Faith Mason

quadrille

Publishing Director: Sarah Lavelle
Editorial Assistant: Harriet Webster
Copy Editor: Corinne Masciocchi
Series Designer: Gemma Hayden
Designer: Tammy Kerr
Food Stylist and Recipe Writer: Rosie Reynolds
Photographer: Faith Mason
Food Stylist Assistants: Esther Clark and Jess Dennison
Prop Stylist: Alexander Breeze
Production Controller: Tom Moore
Production Director: Vincent Smith

Published in 2018 by Quadrille, an imprint of Hardie Grant Publishing

Quadrille
52–54 Southwark Street
London SE1 1UN
quadrille.com

Cataloguing in Publication Data: a catalogue record for this book is available from the British Library.

ISBN: 978 1 78713 119 4

Printed in China

CONTENTS

INTRODUCTION

Rumour has it that the sandwich was less the invention of the 4th Earl of Sandwich, but more of an accidental brainwave, when he became peckish during a game of cards and asked for some meat to be placed between a couple of slices of bread. The magic that happened became the sandwich.

The sandwich is so many things to so many people: breakfast, elevenses, packed lunch al desko… A portable, hand-held lunch on the go, a sit-down dinner, end of dinner wiper-upper of all the good stuff left over on your plate after a meal; late-night fridge-raid fodder or sophisticated high tea.

Sandwiches can be savoury – ranging from bacon at breakfast to Roman-style sausage and broccoli buns (page 27), Mexican-style chicken tortas (page 77) or the ultimate cheese burgers (page 49). They can also be sweet, such as the showstopper Victoria sponge (page 150) – light, fluffy cakes layered with softly whipped cream and jam.

There aren't many ingredients that can't be worked into a sandwich to delicious effect – from a bunch of carrots to whole joints of meat. The sandwich comes in many forms, not only on traditional sliced bread, but in buttery brioche rolls; soft floury buns; dark, chewy rye bread; pillowy waffles; pita pockets and even whole hollowed-out loaves of bread.

This book is an ode to the Earl, a celebration of the lunchtime staple. A collection of the poshest, most delicious sandwich recipes, designed to inspire you and to provide a sandwich idea for all occasions.

BUILDING YOUR

★

SANDWICH

Choosing your bread

As a rule of thumb, always use the best bread you can find; you should want to eat the bread you use with or without the filling. Not only is your bread the vehicle, it also plays a big role in providing flavour and texture.

Next step, think about what you will be 'sandwiching' and whether your bread is appropriate. Soft, moist or saucy fillings generally need a more robust bread with a denser texture to help maintain structure and a good crust to contrast with the soft centre of the sandwich.

Crisp, crunchy and drier fillings can be housed between slices of softer, doughier bread, where the textures will complement each other perfectly. Obviously, if you are a white-sliced kind of gal or guy, then only this will do. Always go with what you love.

Spreading your bread

Not only does a slick of butter, mayo, mustard, dressing or sauce spread on your bread add a layer of flavour to your sandwich, it also adds texture and moisture. Importantly, your choice of spread will create a barrier between the bread and filling, preventing your sandwich from becoming soggy.

Whatever spread you choose, take it right to the edges – no dry corners please. Your last mouthful should be as good as your first.

To toast or not to toast

Some sandwiches call out for the bread to be soft and yielding. When the bread can hold its own against the filling, leave it dense, doughy and untoasted – I'm thinking of the Twice-fried hand-cut chip butties (page 110).

If your sandwich is on the moist side and you don't want the bread to soak up all the juices, a gentle toast under a hot grill or a few minutes in a griddle pan will help the bread to keep its integrity, and stop it collapsing into a soggy mess in front of your eyes. Toasting and griddling your bread also adds a delicious nutty, toasty flavour to your sandwich.

Choosing your filling

This book is packed full of posh recipe delights designed to give you the ultimate sandwich experience. Bread has been chosen for its texture and taste, but so that it complements the filling rather than overshadowing it or leaving the filling to sing alone.

Spreads and fillings have been chosen for taste, texture and deliciousness; accompaniments, such as pickles and slaws, for their supporting role to the main event.

A few hints if you do decide to get experimental with your fillings:

• Something bitter is great balanced with something sweet
• Creamy needs a little acid hit
• Crunchy loves squidgy softness
• Salty goes so well with sweet
• Fatty needs something healthy
• Healthy always needs something indulgent

If you are not going to eat your sandwich immediately, wet ingredients such as tomatoes, lettuce, slaws and pickles can be stored separately and added when you are ready to serve.

How to eat your sandwich

Most sandwiches can be eaten with your hands, pulled from a paper bag, wrapped in foil or plastic wrap, sliced, diced and cut into wedges for a picnic, a buffet spread or your packed lunchbox.

Posh sandwiches sometimes require an accessory to facilitate the eating thereof. Serve afternoon tea on dainty plates, sandwich cakes with a little fork, and always have a pile of napkins at the ready for messy fingers.

Most importantly, take the time to sit and enjoy your sandwich. It is posh, after all.

MEAT

★

SANDWICHES

EGG, MUSHROOM,
★
SAUSAGE & SPINACH

Feel virtuous first thing in the morning eating a sandwich packed with delicious greens. It may even go some way to dissolving the ills of the night before.

SERVES 2

TAKES 20 minutes

6 good-quality sausages
2 tbsp olive oil, plus a drizzle
4 chestnut mushrooms, sliced
1 garlic clove, finely chopped
¼ tsp chilli flakes
100g (3½oz) baby leaf spinach
2 medium eggs
4 slices crusty bread
butter, for spreading
salt and black pepper

Heat a large, non-stick frying pan over a medium heat. Rub the sausages with a little oil, then cook for 15 minutes, turning frequently, until golden and cooked through. Remove from the pan and keep warm in a low oven.

Add 1 tablespoon of the oil to the pan. Increase the heat and fry the mushrooms for 5 minutes until golden. Add the garlic and chilli flakes and fry for 1 minute, or until fragrant. Stir in the spinach and allow the heat of the pan to just wilt the leaves. Tip out onto a plate and keep warm.

Wipe out the pan using kitchen paper and return to the heat. Pour in the remaining oil, then crack the eggs into the pan and cook to your liking. To assemble the sandwiches, lightly toast the bread on both sides under a hot grill, spread with butter, then pile on the mushrooms, spinach, sausages and a fried egg. Season, sandwich with the remaining bread and serve immediately.

Pictured on previous page (right)

SAUSAGE, EGG &
★
CHEESE

The drive-through experience I am sure we've all had
– without having to leave the house!

SERVES 2

TAKES 20 minutes

6 good-quality sausages
1 tbsp olive oil, plus a drizzle
2 medium eggs
4 slices crusty white bread
75g (2½oz) mature Cheddar
   cheese, sliced

Heat a large, non-stick frying pan over a medium heat. Rub the sausages with a little oil, then cook for 15 minutes, turning frequently, until golden and cooked through. Push the sausages to one side and heat a drizzle more oil. Crack the eggs into the pan and cook to your liking.

Meanwhile, lightly toast the bread on both sides, lay the cheese slices on two of the slices of bread and flash under a hot grill until melted. Remove and pile on the sausages and a fried egg. Sandwich with the remaining slices of toast.

Pictured on page 12 (centre)

THE FULL
★
ENGLISH

Just like the saying goes, 'eat breakfast like a king, lunch like a prince and dinner like a pauper', this sandwich is packed with everything you need to start your day the right way.

SERVES 2

TAKES 30 minutes

4 good-quality sausages
2 tbsp olive oil, plus a drizzle
4 rashers smoked streaky bacon
2 tomatoes, halved
2 medium eggs
2 English muffins
butter, for spreading

Heat a large, non-stick frying pan over a medium–high heat. Rub the sausages with a little oil, then cook for 15 minutes, turning frequently, until golden and cooked through. Five minutes before the end of cooking, add the bacon to the pan and cook until golden and starting to crisp.

Push the sausages and bacon to one side to keep warm and add a drizzle more oil. Add the tomatoes, cut-side down, and cook for 3 minutes. Remove everything from the pan and keep warm.

Pour in the remaining oil and fry the eggs to your liking. To assemble, split the muffins in half and lightly toast under a hot grill, then spread with butter. Split the sausages lengthways to stop them rolling out and lay them on the muffin bases. Top with bacon, tomato and a fried egg. Sandwich with the top halves of the muffins and serve.

Pictured on page 12 (left)

PICCALILLI WITH HAM & CHEESE
★
PLOUGHMAN'S

Piccalilli is a British version of an Indian pickle. The crunchy vegetable pickle, lightly spiced in sweet and salty brine, has a punchy flavour that will cut through the richness of any meat or cheese.

SERVES 4

TAKES 20 minutes, plus 2 hours cooling

For the piccalilli
350ml (12fl oz) cider vinegar
3 garlic cloves, finely sliced
1 small red chilli, finely sliced
1.5-cm (½-in) piece ginger, peeled
    and cut into matchsticks
2 tsp ground turmeric
1 tsp salt
5 tbsp granulated sugar
½ small cauliflower (about
    150g/5½oz), broken into
    small florets
1½ tsp English mustard
1 tbsp plain (all-purpose) flour
10 small silverskin pickled onions
1 turnip, cut into 1-cm
    (⅜-in) cubes
½ carrot, cut into 1-cm
    (⅜-in) cubes
⅓ cucumber, halved lengthways,
    deseeded and roughly diced

Start by making the piccalilli. In a medium pan, add the cider vinegar, garlic, chilli, ginger, turmeric, salt and sugar. Bring to the boil, then simmer for 5 minutes. Add the cauliflower florets and cook for 2 minutes more. Mix the mustard and flour in a small heatproof bowl with 3 tablespoons of the hot brine from the pan. Stir to form a smooth paste, then add a further 5 tablespoons of cooking liquid and mix well.

Stir the mustard mixture into the brine pan, then cook on a high heat for 2 minutes, or until thickened and glossy. Remove from the heat, then stir in the pickled onions, turnip, carrot and cucumber, and allow to cool completely, about 2–3 hours (or overnight if possible). Ladle into a couple of sealable and sterilized glass jars, or store in a lidded plastic container in the fridge for up to two weeks. (Be warned – the turmeric may dye your chosen container yellow...)

ingredients and method continue overleaf...

★ ★ ★ ★ ★ ★ ★ ★ ★ ★ ★ ★ ★ ★ ★ ★

★ ★

HAM AND CHEESE PLOUGHMAN'S
continued...

8 slices crusty wholemeal bread
butter, for spreading
200g (7oz) thick-cut ham
150g (5½oz) mature Cheddar
    cheese, sliced

celery sticks, cherry tomatoes
    and apples, to serve

When you're ready to assemble your sandwich,
lay four slices of crusty bread on a board, spread
generously with butter, and then layer over the
ham and cheese. Generously spoon some of your
home-made piccalilli over the ham and cheese then
pop the remaining slices of bread on top.

Serve with crunchy celery sticks, cherry tomatoes
and an apple on the side. The perfect lunchtime
snack for a walk in the British countryside.

STUFFED

★

PICNIC LOAF

You can make this mega sandwich up to two days in advance and chill until required. Perfect for a picnic or packed lunches. Use the scooped-out bread centre to make crispy croutons for salads or soup.

SERVES 4–6

TAKES 30 minutes, plus standing

1 x 400g (14oz) round crusty loaf
2 tbsp green pesto
2 tbsp good-quality mayonnaise
75g (2½oz) sliced fennel salami
75g (2½oz) roasted peppers from a jar, drained
75g (2½oz) chargrilled artichokes in oil, drained
50g (1¾oz) sun-blushed tomatoes, drained
25g (scant 1oz) Parmesan cheese
large handful basil leaves
150g (5½oz) mozzarella cheese, drained
80g (2¾oz) Parma ham
large handful rocket (arugula)
freshly ground black pepper

Use a bread knife to cut off the top of the loaf about two-thirds of the way up. Scoop out most of the doughy middle and a layer of the lid, leaving a bread shell. Mix the pesto and mayo together and spread inside the base and lid of the loaf right up the sides.

Line the base of the loaf with the salami. Roughly chop the peppers, artichokes and tomatoes. Mix these together and spread half on top of the salami. Use a potato peeler to shave half the Parmesan cheese over the top, then scatter over a few torn basil leaves.

Pat the mozzarella dry on kitchen paper, then slice. Lay a single layer on top of the basil, followed by all the Parma ham and half the rocket – flatten down with the back of your hand as you go. Repeat with another layer of chopped vegetables, more Parmesan and mozzarella, and keep going until you have used up all the ingredients. Season each layer with a twist of black pepper.

Replace the lid of the loaf, gently press together and wrap tightly in plastic wrap. Chill for 2–3 hours. Cut into generous wedges to serve.

MEATBALL
★
SUB

These saucy sandwiches can get quite messy, so you want to assemble them just before you serve. If you like your subs fully loaded you can add salad, fried onions or a handful of twice-fried hand-cut chips (page 110).

SERVES 4

TAKES 45 minutes

500g (1lb 2oz) minced (ground) beef
1 onion, grated
2 garlic cloves, crushed
1 tsp chilli flakes
1 tsp dried oregano
1 tsp smoked paprika
1 tsp ground cumin
handful parsley, finely chopped
3 tbsp fresh breadcrumbs
25g (scant 1oz) Parmesan cheese, grated
1 large egg, lightly beaten
salt and black pepper
olive oil
680g (1lb 8oz) rustic passata
4 submarine rolls, or 1 large baguette
75g (2½oz) strong Cheddar cheese, grated

Preheat the oven to 200°C/400°F/gas 6.

Tip the mince into a large bowl and add the onion, garlic, spices and most of the parsley, reserving a little for garnish. Add the breadcrumbs, Parmesan, egg and plenty of seasoning. Massage together with your hands for 2 minutes – this will combine the ingredients and help the meatballs to stay together as they cook.

Use lightly oiled hands to divide the meat mixture into 16 walnut-sized balls. Lightly grease a baking dish with oil and sit the meatballs in the dish. Bake for 15 minutes.

Remove from the oven and pour over the passata. Give everything a stir, then return to the oven and bake for a further 15 minutes, or until the meatballs are cooked through and the sauce is bubbling and thickened.

To serve, split the sub rolls in half and spoon in four saucy meatballs, reserving any excess sauce for serving. Top with the Cheddar, flash under a hot grill until the cheese is melted and sprinkle with the remaining parsley.

THE NEW YORK
★
REUBEN

The classic New York deli sandwich loaded with pastrami,
a sharp Russian dressing, melted Swiss cheese and tangy
sauerkraut. Serve with some fries for a satisfying dinner.

 SERVES 2

TAKES 20 minutes

For the Russian dressing
2½ tbsp mayonnaise
1 tbsp tomato ketchup
¼ tsp hot sauce (I used Tabasco)
¼ tsp Worcestershire sauce
1 shallot, finely diced
2 tsp creamed horseradish
¼ tsp paprika

4 slices good white bread
160g (5¾oz) sliced pastrami
2 slices Swiss cheese
125g (4½oz) sauerkraut, drained
4 dill pickles, drained and thinly
   sliced lengthways

Start by making the Russian dressing. In a bowl,
mix half the mayo with all the the ketchup, hot
sauce, Worcestershire sauce, shallot, horseradish
and paprika. Spread the remaining tablespoon of
mayo across the four slices of bread, then flip and
spread the other side of the bread with the Russian
dressing. Layer up the pastrami, cheese, sauerkraut
and pickles on two slices, then top with the
remaining bread, mayo-side up.

Heat a large, non-stick frying pan over a medium–
high heat. Add the sandwiches – the mayo will
help the bread crisp up. Press down with a spatula
and cook for 2 minutes, or until golden. Flip the
sandwiches carefully with a spatula and fry for a
further 2 minutes. Serve immediately.

ROMAN-STYLE SAUSAGE & BROCCOLI BUNS

The broccoli becomes melt-in-the-mouth tender and the bread soaks up all the delicious juices. These sandwiches are a meal in one glorious handful.

SERVES 4

TAKES 20 minutes

200g (7oz) Tenderstem broccoli
1 tbsp olive oil
8 good-quality sausages
1 onion, sliced
½ tsp chilli flakes
1 tsp fennel seeds
a knob of butter
4 ciabatta rolls, or other crusty
   bread rolls

Cook the broccoli in a pan of boiling salted water for 3 minutes. Drain, reserving about half a cup of the cooking liquid. Cool the broccoli under cold running water to stop it cooking any further. Drain and set aside.

Heat the oil in a large, non-stick frying pan over a medium–high heat. Cook the sausages, turning them frequently for about 10 minutes, or until they are browned all over. Add the onion, chilli flakes and fennel seeds, and fry for 5 minutes until lightly golden and starting to soften. Tip in the cooked broccoli and heat through. Increase the heat, pour in about 3 tablespoons of the cooking water and the butter, and shake the pan to emulsify the juices. Remove from the heat.

To serve, split the bread rolls in half, divide the sausages and broccoli equally between the buns and spoon over the onion and any pan juices.

SPICY SALAMI
★
PIZZA SLIDERS

These pizza sliders can be made with large or small rolls. Perfect for a party, you can go mad with the fillings – ham and pineapple is a great nostalgic trip. Bring the hot rolls to the table and let your guests pull them apart.

MAKES 12 rolls

TAKES 30 minutes

50g (1¾oz) soft unsalted butter, plus extra for greasing
1 fat garlic clove, crushed
1 tsp chilli flakes
12 mini bread rolls
150g (5½oz) mozzarella cheese, grated
½ x 400g (14oz) can chopped tomatoes with herbs
2 tbsp tomato purée
handful basil leaves, torn, plus extra for garnish
salt and black pepper
16 slices spicy pepperoni sausage
1 small red chilli, sliced
25g (scant 1oz) pitted black olives, roughly chopped
25g (scant 1oz) Parmesan cheese, grated

First make the garlic butter. Melt the butter in a small pan over a low heat. Remove from the heat and mix in the garlic and chilli flakes, then set aside.

Preheat the oven to 200°C/400°F/gas 6. Without separating the rolls, slice them in half so that you have one giant top and bottom.

Use the extra butter to lightly grease a baking dish large enough to fit all the rolls. Place the bottom halves of the rolls in the dish. Scatter over half the mozzarella and bake for 5 minutes to melt the cheese and firm up the base.

Sieve the tomatoes to remove any excess liquid. Mix the tomatoes with the purée and stir in the basil, season and spoon over the melted cheese. Top with the pepperoni, chilli and olives. Cover with the remaining mozzarella, then pop the giant bread roll lid on top.

Brush the tops of the rolls with the garlic butter and sprinkle over the Parmesan. Bake for 10–15 minutes until the rolls are golden and the cheese is oozing. If the buns are getting too much colour cover them with foil. Remove from the oven and scatter with basil leaves. Devour while hot.

CUBANOS

Cubanos are piled full of cooked meats and Swiss cheese, sandwiched in crispy-on-the-outside, soft-in-the-middle bread flattened in a hot pan until crisp and melting. Serve with a little sweetened Cuban coffee for a real treat.

SERVES 2

TAKES 20 minutes

2 small baguettes or panini loaves
2 tbsp good-quality mayonnaise
2 tsp Dijon mustard, plus extra
  to serve
125g (4½oz) sliced roast pork,
  or pork leftovers
4 slices Swiss cheese
125g (4½oz) honey-roast ham
light olive oil, for frying
mustard and pickles, to serve

Halve the baguettes lengthways. In a bowl, mix the mayo and mustard together and spread on the cut sides of the bread. Layer up the roast pork, cheese and ham, and sandwich together with the top halves of the bread.

Heat the oil in a large, non-stick frying pan over a medium–high heat. Put the sandwiches in, lightly grease the underside of a heavy-based pan and use it to weigh down the sandwiches so they are in complete contact with the pan. Cook for 2 minutes, or until crisp and golden.

Remove the top pan, carefully flip the sandwiches over and continue to cook with the heavy pan on top for 2 minutes.

Remove the sandwiches from the pan and slice. Serve with pickles and extra mustard, if liked.

PICKLE SLAW, CURRY MAYO &
PANKO PORK

This sandwich takes the delicious textures and taste of katsu curry and rolls it all up into one mouth-wateringly good sandwich. The pickles cut through the rich, crispy crumb of the pork and complement the creamy mayo.

SERVES 2

TAKES 45 minutes

For the panko-covered pork chops
1 large egg
4 tbsp plain (all-purpose) flour
salt and black pepper
5 tbsp panko breadcrumbs
2 boneless pork loin steaks, fat trimmed
light olive oil, for frying

For the pickle slaw
1 tbsp pickled ginger, shredded
1 large carrot, cut into matchsticks
4 radishes, cut into matchsticks
1 tbsp clear honey
½ small garlic clove

For the curry mayo
3 tbsp good-quality mayonnaise
2 tsp hot curry powder
drizzle of clear honey

2 large soft white rolls
¼ Chinese leaf lettuce, shredded

Prepare the pork chops. Lightly beat the egg in a shallow bowl. Tip the flour onto a plate and season. Tip the breadcrumbs onto another plate. Lay the pork chops between two sheets of plastic wrap and bash with a rolling pin to flatten. Dip the pork in the flour, coat all over, then shake off any excess. Repeat with the egg wash and then the breadcrumbs.

Preheat oven to 180°C/350°F/gas 4. Heat a glug of oil in a large, non-stick frying pan over a medium heat. Fry the pork chops for 3–5 minutes on each side, until golden and crisp. Transfer to a baking sheet and cook for a further 8 minutes in the oven.

Meanwhile, make the pickle. Add the pickled ginger to a bowl with 1 teaspoon of the pickling liquid, along with the carrot and radishes. Stir in the honey and garlic, and leave to stand for 5 minutes.

For the curry mayo, mix the mayonnaise, curry powder and honey together and season.

Halve the bread rolls and spread with the curry mayo. Lay the lettuce on the bottom halves. Remove the pork from the oven, thickly slice and lay it on top. Pile the pickle slaw on top of the crispy pork and sandwich with the top halves of the rolls.

SHOESTRING FRIES WITH
HAM & EGG

Use the best ham you can find and duck eggs for this posh sandwich. The shoestring fries add crunch and turn this into a sarnie fit for a rather fancy, naughty-but-nice meal.

SERVES 2

TAKES 20 minutes

1 large Maris Piper potato
500ml (17fl oz) sunflower oil,
    for shallow frying
fine salt
2 duck eggs (or extra-large free
    range chicken eggs)
2 thick slices hand-carved ham
For the spiced mayo
2 tbsp good-quality mayonnaise
1 tbsp tamarind paste
1 tsp Worcestershire sauce
1 tbsp smooth mango pickle

2 large white rolls

Peel the potato and use a julienne peeler to cut it into very thin matchsticks. Lay on a clean tea towel and pat dry to remove any excess water. Heat the oil in a high-sided saucepan over a medium–high heat. Test whether the oil is hot enough by adding a potato stick – it should bubble and cook within 4–5 minutes. Cook the matchsticks in batches until crisp and lightly golden – do not allow them to take on too much colour. Remove with a slotted spoon and drain on kitchen paper. Sprinkle with salt.

Mix all of the spiced mayo ingredients together in a bowl and set aside.

Take a couple of tablespoons of oil from the chip pan and heat in a large, non-stick frying pan over a medium–high heat. Crack the eggs into the hot oil, being careful not to splash yourself, and cook to your liking.

Split the bread rolls in half, spread the cut sides with the spiced mayo and lay a slice of ham on the base of each roll. Slide a fried egg on top and a handful of shoestring fries. Top with the other half of the roll and serve immediately.

HORSERADISH CREAM &
★
ROAST BEEF

It's such a treat to roast a joint of meat for sandwiches. These really are the poshest of the posh and would be wonderful served on a summer's day in the garden alongside a big green salad.

 SERVES 6

TAKES 1 hour 30 minutes

1.3kg (3lb) boned joint of beef
   (I used topside)
1–2 tbsp vegetable oil
2 tbsp Dijon mustard
2 tbsp cracked black pepper
sea salt flakes
For the horseradish cream
5 tbsp grated horseradish (fresh
   or jarred is fine)
5 tbsp crème fraîche

crusty white bread, sliced
handful of watercress

Preheat the oven to 180°C/350°C fan/gas 5.

Pat the beef dry with kitchen paper and allow it to come to room temperature. Heat the oil in a large, heavy casserole dish and brown the meat all over, turning with tongs every couple of minutes, until a nice crust forms on the meat – it will take about 10 minutes. Brush the outside of the meat with 1 tablespoon of the mustard, then sprinkle with the black pepper, pushing it into the mustard so that it sticks. Season with salt.

Place in the oven and roast for 35–40 minutes. Remove from the casserole dish and transfer to a chopping board. Cover loosely with foil and leave to rest for 15 minutes.

Meanwhile, make the horseradish cream. Mix the horseradish with the crème fraîche and the remaining tablespoon of mustard.

Carve the beef into thin slices, spread the bread with horseradish cream, pile with beef and any resting juices, and top with a handful of watercress. Serve immediately.

PORK BAO
★
BUNS

Bao buns are just like making normal bread rolls, except they are steamed rather than baked. Steaming gives them a unique shiny exterior and a toothsome spring.

🍴 MAKES 12 buns

⏰ TAKES 1 hour, plus rising and proving

500g (1lb 2oz) plain (all-purpose) flour, plus extra for dusting
1 tsp baking powder (soda)
7g sachet fast-action yeast
1 tbsp caster (superfine) sugar
1 tsp fine salt
2 tbsp sunflower oil, plus extra for greasing

For the filling
1kg (2lb 4oz) pork belly slices, halved
240ml (8½fl oz) hoisin sauce
2 tbsp chilli sauce
1 tbsp dark soy sauce

6 spring onions (scallions), shredded
1 cucumber, deseeded and cut into thin strips
handful salted peanuts, roughly chopped

Lightly grease two baking sheets with oil. Cut out 24 x 10cm (½ x 4in) squares of baking parchment.

Combine the flour, baking powder, yeast, sugar and salt in a large mixing bowl. Make a well in the flour, add the oil, then gradually add 250ml (8½fl oz) of warm water, stirring to form a soft, sticky dough. Tip the dough onto a floured surface and knead for 10 minutes, until you have a soft shiny dough. Transfer to a lightly greased bowl, cover and leave for 1 hour in a warm spot until doubled in size.

Tip the dough onto a floured surface and knead briefly to remove excess air. Divide the dough into 12 equal pieces. Shape each into a ball, covering with a clean tea towel as you go to prevent drying. Use a rolling pin to roll each ball into an oval about 15cm (6in) long, then brush the surface of the dough with oil. Lay a piece of baking parchment over the bottom half of the oval. Fold the top half of the bun over the paper. Put the bun on a square

method continues overleaf...

★ ★ ★ ★ ★ ★ ★ ★ ★ ★ ★ ★ ★ ★ ★

PORK BAO BUNS

continued...

of parchment, then transfer to a tray. Repeat with the remaining buns. Cover loosely with a clean tea towel and leave to prove for a further 1 hour, or until doubled in size.

Meanwhile, prepare the filling. Put the pork belly slices in a baking dish and cover with the hoisin sauce, chilli sauce and soy. Cover and leave to marinate for at least 1 hour. When you are ready to cook, preheat the grill to medium–high. Lift the pork belly out of the marinade, shaking off any excess and reserving the sauce in the bowl. Lay on a flat baking sheet and grill for 20 minutes, turning frequently throughout cooking, until the fat is bubbling and the meat is charred in places. Remove, cover with foil and keep warm in the oven. Pour the reserved marinade into a small pan and heat gently.

Heat a large steamer over a large saucepan filled with 5cm (2in) boiling water. Lift the buns by the paper they sit on and steam in batches (depending on the size of your steamer) for 10–12 minutes, or until shiny and puffed up. Open the buns up, discard the central piece of paper and fill with pork belly, a spoonful of sauce, spring onions, cucumber slices and a sprinkling of peanuts.

APPLE PICKLE WITH CRISPY
★
PORK BELLY

Crispy pork belly needs no introduction. The soft, meltingly
tender pork and crisp crackling sit so well in a sandwich
with sliced roasted apple and a spoon of tart apple pickle.
This will definitely keep you coming back for more.

SERVES 4–6

TAKES 3 hours 30 minutes

2kg (4lb 8oz) pork belly, skin scored
    (ask your butcher to do this)
2 tbsp fennel seeds
2 tsp chilli flakes
1 tsp fine salt
1 tbsp olive oil, plus a drizzle
3 sprigs rosemary, leaves stripped
    and finely chopped
5 sage leaves, finely chopped
2 garlic cloves, finely chopped
juice 1 lemon
150ml (5fl oz) apple juice
2 eating apples, cored
For the apple pickle
1 small red onion, finely sliced
1 tbsp clear honey
salt and black pepper
1 small eating apple, cored and
    cut into matchsticks

6 floury white rolls

Preheat the oven to 220°C/425°F/gas 7.

Put the pork belly in a deep roasting dish. Crush
the fennel seeds, chilli flakes and salt in a pestle and
mortar until you have a fine powder. Rub the pork
with the oil, then massage the spice powder into
the skin and flesh. Put the rosemary, sage and garlic
into the pestle and mortar with half the lemon
juice, and bash until you have a coarse paste. Rub
the paste all over the flesh side of the pork. Roast
for 30 minutes.

Reduce the oven temperature to 160°C/325°F/
gas 3. Add the apple juice to the dish, cover with
foil, then return to the oven for 2½ hours. Check
halfway through cooking and top up with a splash
of apple juice or water if the roasting dish is drying
out. Thirty minutes before the end of cooking, cut
the apples into wedges and toss with a little oil,
then add to the pan, stir to coat in the meat juices,
re-cover and continue cooking.

method continues overleaf...

★ ★ ★ ★ ★ ★ ★ ★ ★ ★ ★ ★ ★ ★ ★ ★

★ ★

CRISPY PORK BELLY
continued...

To make the apple pickle, put the onion in a bowl and squeeze over the juice of the remaining lemon half. Drizzle with the honey, season and set aside for 5 minutes. Stir through the apple sticks and leave to stand for 1 minute before serving.

Remove the pork from the oven and separate the crackling from the top of the belly joint using a sharp knife. If the crackling is not crisp, flash it under a hot grill until bubbled up and crisp – keep watching all the time as it burns very easily!

Slice the pork and split the bread rolls. Pile the pork onto the rolls with a couple of apple wedges and a spoonful of the apple pickle. Skim any fat off the pan juices and transfer to a jug for pouring over or dunking the sandwiches into. Cut the crackling into strips and serve alongside the sandwiches.

SWEET & SOUR
★
LAMB KOFTA PITTA

These fragrant lamb patties work brilliantly as part
of a modern mezze meal. The sweet and sour salad
cuts through the richness of the lamb, making
these pittas totally moreish.

SERVES 4

TAKES 30 minutes

500g (1lb 2oz) minced
   (ground) lamb
2 tsp ground cinnamon
2 tsp cumin
2 tsp ground coriander
2 tsp paprika
bunch mint, finely chopped
bunch coriander (cilantro),
   finely chopped
1 tbsp vegetable oil, for greasing
For the salad
½ red onion, finely chopped
1 red chilli
1 large carrot, grated
juice ½ lemon
1 tbsp pomegranate molasses
salt and black pepper

4 tbsp good-quality mayonnaise
2 tbsp harissa
8 mini pittas

Put the lamb into a large bowl, add the spices, most
of the mint and most of the coriander, reserving
about 1 tablespoon of each for the salad. Massage
together with your hands for 2 minutes; this will
combine the ingredients and help the patties stay
together as they cook.

Divide the lamb mixture into eight equal portions.
Using damp hands, shape the meat into rugby ball-
shaped patties. Grease a baking sheet with a little
oil and lay the patties on top. Set aside.

To make the salad, mix the onion, chilli and carrot
with the lemon juice and pomegranate molasses.
Gently stir in the reserved herbs and some
seasoning. In a small bowl, mix the mayo with the
harissa and set aside.

Heat the grill to high. Cook the patties for 8
minutes, turning frequently, until golden and
cooked through. To serve, split the pittas and heat
under the hot grill. When warmed, spread with the
harissa mayo, sit a kofta inside and top with salad.

OLIVE, CHEESE & SALAMI
★
MUFFULETTA

This is the quintessential, New Orleans layered sandwich.
Use the best ingredients you can find and allow the
sandwich to stand before serving to let the tangy olive
spread soak into the bread.

 SERVES 6

TAKES 20 minutes,
plus standing

For the olive spread
100g (3½oz) pimento-stuffed
    green olives
100g (3½oz) Kalamata olives
2 tbsp capers
3 hot pickled peppers, finely
    chopped
1 garlic clove, crushed
2 tbsp olive oil
2 tbsp fresh oregano leaves, finely
    chopped, or 1 tsp dried
salt and black pepper

350g (12oz) focaccia
180g (6oz) mortadella
8 slices Emmenthal, sliced
90g (3¼oz) Italian salami
100g (3½oz) Gruyère, sliced

Start by making the olive spread. Put the stuffed
green olives, Kalamata olives, capers and pickled
peppers on a chopping board and run over the lot
with a sharp knife backwards and forwards until
everything is very finely chopped. Scrape into a
bowl and add 2 tablespoons of the pickling liquid
from the peppers. Stir in the garlic, oil and chopped
oregano. Season and set aside.

Cut the focaccia in half lengthways and lay cut
side-up on a board. Spread generously with olive
spread. Layer the bottom half of the bread with
half the mortadella, followed by Emmenthal and
salami layers, the Gruyère and finally the remaining
mortadella. Sandwich with the top half of the
focaccia. Wrap the whole thing tightly in plastic
wrap, sit on a board and weigh down with a baking
sheet. Chill for at least 30 minutes and slice before
serving. Goes especially well with a cold beer.

THE ULTIMATE
★
CHEESE BURGER

Just because the burger is a classic doesn't mean it has to be classy. Go mad and fill your burger with whatever tickles your fancy, from a fried egg to crispy bacon. The only rule is there must be a patty between those buns.

SERVES 4

TAKES 30 minutes

500g (1lb 2oz) 20% fat minced (ground) beef
½ tsp fine salt
black pepper
2 tbsp vegetable oil
1 large onion, thinly sliced
4 strong Cheddar cheese slices
4 sesame burger buns

For the burger sauce
4 tbsp good-quality mayonnaise
2 tsp tomato ketchup
1 tsp Dijon mustard
½ small garlic clove, crushed
½ tsp paprika
3 sweet dill pickles, finely chopped

½ iceberg lettuce, shredded
2 ripe tomatoes, sliced

Start by making the burger sauce. In a bowl, mix together the mayo, ketchup, mustard, garlic, paprika and pickles (plus a bit of the pickling liquid). Season and chill until ready to use.

To make the burgers, put the beef and salt into a bowl with a generous grinding of black pepper. Mix with your hands for 5 minutes to break down the fibres in the meat – this will help your burgers stay together. Divide into four equal pieces, shape into patties and rub each with a little oil. Season the outside of each patty with more fine sea salt.

Heat a large, heavy, non-stick frying pan over a high heat. Cook the burgers for 8 minutes, flipping every 2 minutes. At the halfway point, add a drizzle more oil and fry the onion, stirring to coat in the oil, until starting to colour and just soften slightly. Push the onion to one side and lay a cheese slice on top of each burger, allowing the heat of the meat and the pan to melt the cheese.

Split the buns and lightly toast the cut sides under a hot grill. Spread the bottoms with burger sauce and add some lettuce and tomato slices. Top with a juicy burger and a spoonful of fried onion. Sandwich with the burger bun tops and serve.

RARE STEAK

★

BANH MI

The lightly pickled vegetables are the perfect foil for the rich rare steak, and the crisp baguette is the perfect vessel for this traditional Vietnamese–French-inspired sandwich.

SERVES 2

TAKES 40 minutes

2 tbsp soy sauce
2 garlic cloves, finely chopped
1 sirloin steak (about 200g/7oz),
    fat removed
2 small white baguettes
2 tbsp good-quality mayonnaise
1½ tsp Sriracha chilli sauce
1 tsp vegetable oil
For the pickles
2 tbsp caster (superfine) sugar
2 tbsp rice wine vinegar
½ tbsp fish sauce
1 small carrot, peeled and cut
    into matchsticks
⅓ cucumber, halved lengthways,
    seeds removed, cut into
    matchsticks
4 radishes, cut into matchsticks
small handful coriander (cilantro)

Mix the soy and garlic in a wide shallow bowl, then add the steak. Marinate for 20 minutes, turning halfway to ensure both sides are fully coated.

Split the baguettes lengthways, leaving them slightly attached at one edge. Pull out most of the fluffy middle. In a small bowl, mix together the mayo and Sriracha, then set aside.

Meanwhile, make the pickles. In a large bowl, mix the sugar, vinegar and fish sauce until the sugar has dissolved. Add the carrot, cucumber and radishes to the dressing, toss to coat and leave to stand for 5 minutes.

Heat a non-stick frying pan over a high heat. Remove the steak from the marinade, pat dry with kitchen paper, then rub all over with the oil. Place the steak in the pan and cook for 1½ minutes each side. Transfer to a board and allow to rest for 10 minutes.

Spread the baguettes with Sriracha mayo, thinly slice the steak and divide between the baguettes. Drain the pickles in a colander, then pile on top with some coriander. Eat immediately.

POULTRY

★

SANDWICHES

CLASSIC

★

ROAST CHICKEN

Nothing beats freshly roasted, crisp-skinned chicken between two slices of soft fresh bread with a garlicky lemon mayo. Here's the basic filling recipe; three sandwich variations follow.

 SERVES 6

TAKES 1 hour 30 minutes, plus resting

1 large whole chicken
   (about 1.6kg/3lb 8oz)
1 tbsp olive oil
2 lemons, halved
sea salt flakes and black pepper
bunch thyme sprigs
2 garlic bulbs
180g (6oz) good-quality
   mayonnaise

Preheat the oven to 200°C/400°F/gas 6.

Cut a few incisions into the legs of the chicken, then place it in a roasting tin. Rub with oil and squeeze over the juice of 1 lemon, reserving the halves.

Season the skin and the cavity of the chicken with salt. Stuff the juiced lemon halves and thyme inside the cavity, then place the 2 remaining lemon halves and garlic bulbs in the tin. Roast for 35 minutes.

Remove the garlic and roasted lemon halves from the tin then return the chicken to the oven for a further 30 minutes, until the chicken skin is crisp and golden and the juices run clear when the meat is pierced with a sharp knife. Rest for 20 minutes.

When cool enough to handle, remove the lemons from the cavity and squeeze any remaining flesh into a bowl, along with the juice from the roasted lemons. Halve the garlic bulbs, then squeeze the roasted pulp into the lemon juice, discarding the garlic skins. Mash with a fork, then stir in the mayo.

Using two forks, roughly shred the chicken meat and skin, leaving some big chunks. Stir any collected chicken juices into the mayo.

CLASSIC

★

ROAST CHICKEN BLT

The holy trilogy of BLT meets the best roast chicken
you might ever taste, with creamy avocado – there is just
so much to love about this sandwich.

🍴 SERVES 6

🕐 TAKES 1 hour 30 minutes,
plus resting

1 Classic Roast Chicken & garlicky
lemon mayo (see opposite)
12 rashers smoked streaky bacon
2 large ciabatta loaves
2 ripe avocados, halved, stoned,
peeled and sliced
½ iceberg lettuce, shredded
3 ripe tomatoes, sliced

Make a Classic Roast Chicken and garlicky lemon
mayo, as per the recipe opposite.

While the chicken is resting, grill the bacon until
golden and crisp. Split the ciabatta loaves in half
lengthways and spread generously with garlicky
lemon mayo. Pile the chicken into the loaves,
followed by a couple of rashers of bacon, slices of
avocado, some lettuce and tomato. Sandwich with
the remaining bread and serve immediately.

Pictured on page 52 (top)

CLASSIC ROAST CHICKEN & ★ CHORIZO

Collect any delicious red oil that melts out of the chorizo
when you fry it and stir it through the mayo for a smoky
kick that works brilliantly with the chicken.

SERVES 6

TAKES 1 hour 30 minutes,
plus resting

1 Classic Roast Chicken & garlicky
   lemon mayo (page 54)
150g (5½oz) chorizo sausage, sliced
1 tsp smoked paprika
12 slices white bread
salt and black pepper

Make a Classic Roast Chicken and garlicky lemon
mayo, as per the recipe on page 54.

Put a large, non-stick frying pan over a medium–
high heat. When the pan is still cold, add the
chorizo and cook for 10–15 minutes, or until the
chorizo is crisp and all of its red oil has melted
out. Drain the chorizo in a sieve over a bowl to
catch any oil. Stir 2 tablespoons of the oil and the
smoked paprika into the garlicky lemon mayo.

Lay the bread slices on a board and spread each
slice with the mayo. Pile the shredded chicken and
chorizo onto half the bread, season and sandwich
with the remaining bread. Serve immediately.

Pictured on page 52 (bottom right)

CLASSIC ROAST CHICKEN &
★
GREEN SALAD

Here, the chicken is the star of the show, adorned with nothing more than a slick of roasted garlicky and lemon mayo and some fresh greens. A true classic.

SERVES 6

TAKES 1 hour 30 minutes, plus resting

1 Classic Roast Chicken & garlicky lemon mayo (page 54)
12 slices good crusty bread
cracked black pepper
150-g (5½-oz) bag mixed leaves

Make a Classic Roast Chicken and garlicky lemon mayo, as per the recipe on page 54.

Lay the bread on a board and spread both sides generously with garlicky lemon mayo. Divide the cooked chicken between six slices and season with a little black pepper. Add handfuls of mixed leaves and close with the remaining bread slices to sandwich together. Cut into wedges and serve.

Pictured on page 52 (bottom left)

CHICKEN

★

PARMIGIANA

Mixing Parmesan into the breadcrumbs to coat the chicken is a winner – the cheese melts, making the crumb extra crispy. Smothered in rich tomato sauce and creamy mozzarella, this sandwich definitely requires an appetite.

SERVES 4

TAKES 45 minutes

For the tomato sauce
1 tbsp olive oil
2 garlic cloves, finely chopped
2 tsp dried oregano
½ tsp chilli flakes
400g (14oz) can chopped tomatoes
2 tbsp tomato purée
pinch sugar
handful basil leaves, chopped
salt and black pepper

2 large skinless chicken breasts
100g (3½oz) plain (all-purpose) flour
2 medium eggs, lightly beaten
100g (3½oz) panko breadcrumbs
1 tsp dried oregano
4 tbsp grated Parmesan cheese
100ml (3½fl oz) vegetable oil

4 ciabatta rolls
125g (4½oz) mozzarella cheese, drained and thinly sliced

Start by making the tomato sauce. Heat the oil in a saucepan over a medium heat. Fry the garlic for 1 minute, then add the oregano, chilli flakes and tomatoes. Stir and simmer for 5 minutes. Stir in the tomato purée, sugar, and season. Cook for a few minutes until the sauce has thickened. Remove from the heat and stir in the chopped basil leaves.

Slice each chicken breast in half horizontally. Sandwich the 4 chicken halves between plastic wrap and bash with a rolling pin to flatten. Put the flour onto a plate and season. Pour the beaten eggs into a shallow bowl. Tip the breadcrumbs, oregano and 3 tablespoons of the Parmesan onto a plate. Coat the chicken pieces in the flour, shaking off any excess. Repeat with the eggwash and the crumb. Heat the oil in a large frying pan over a medium heat. Fry the chicken for 4–6 minutes on each side until golden and crisp. Drain on kitchen paper.

Heat the grill to high. Halve the ciabatta rolls and place the bottoms on an oven tray. Spread over the tomato sauce and layer over the mozzarella. Flash under the grill until just starting to melt. Top each with a crisp chicken escalope and sprinkle with the remaining Parmesan. Sandwich with the top half of the rolls and serve.

SANDWICHES

Created in honour of the coronation of Elizabeth II in 1953, the curried mango mayo and perfectly cooked chicken in this sandwich make for the perfect lunch. Once retro, this British classic is coming back in a BIG WAY.

SERVES 3

TAKES 10 minutes

4 tbsp good-quality mayonnaise
1 heaped tbsp smooth mango
    chutney
2 tsp curry powder
¼ tsp paprika
salt and black pepper
2 cooked chicken breasts (or use
    the Classic Roast Chicken recipe
    on page 54)
2 tbsp toasted flaked almonds
2 tbsp sultanas
3 slices brown bread
3 slices white bread

watercress and crisps (potato
    chips), to serve

In a mixing bowl stir together the mayonnaise, mango chutney, curry powder and paprika. Season to taste.

Shred the chicken breasts and add to the curry mayonnaise with the flaked almonds and sultanas, stirring to combine.

Lay the brown bread on a board and spread with the coronation chicken. Sandwich with the white bread. Cut each sandwich into four triangles. Serve immediately. Makes 12 triangles.

CHICKEN
★
WALDORF SALAD

Inspired by the classic Waldorf salad, crisp apple and celery
add texture to a traditional chicken mayo salad.
A creamy and crunchy delight!

SERVES 4

TAKES 15 minutes

2 cooked skinless chicken breasts
1 small eating apple, finely sliced
2 celery sticks, finely sliced
2 tbsp good-quality mayonnaise
1 tsp Dijon mustard
½ garlic clove, crushed
salt and black pepper
50g (1¾oz) walnuts, toasted and
   roughly chopped
4 slices crusty white bread

Shred the chicken into bite-sized pieces. Transfer
to a bowl and add the apple, celery, mayo, mustard
and garlic. Season and stir to coat in the mayo. At
this point you can cover and chill the mixture until
ready to serve.

When ready to serve, fold through most of the
walnuts into the chicken mixture. Pile the chicken
onto the bread slices and top with extra walnuts.
Serve immediately.

CHIPOTLE SLAW &

★

CRISPY CHICKEN

Chipotle chilli adds a lovely smoky flavour to traditional creamy slaw. You will find chipotle chilli paste in the spice aisle or next to marinades in your local supermarket – just remember, a little goes a long way!

SERVES 4

TAKES 20 minutes

For the chipotle slaw
2 tbsp good-quality mayonnaise
2 tbsp Greek yogurt
1 tbsp chipotle chilli paste
½ small white cabbage
½ small onion, thinly sliced
1 large carrot, coarsely grated
1 tbsp chopped chives

3 tbsp plain (all-purpose) flour
1 tsp smoked paprika
½ tsp mild chilli powder
½ tsp garlic powder
salt and black pepper
4 skin-on boneless chicken thighs
2 tbsp light olive oil

4 brioche rolls
dill pickles, to serve

Start by making the chipotle slaw. In a large bowl, mix the mayo, yogurt and chilli paste together. Season and set aside. Shred the cabbage with a sharp knife or on a mandolin (watch your fingers!) and add it to the dressing bowl. Add the onion and carrot to the bowl, toss to coat in the dressing, then cover and leave to stand. You can make this the day before and chill until ready to serve.

Put the flour on a plate with the paprika, chilli powder and garlic powder. Season well and stir to combine. Dust the chicken thighs in the seasoned flour, patting the flour into the meat.

Heat the oil in a large, non-stick frying pan over a medium heat. Cook the chicken thighs skin-side down for 10 minutes, or until the skin is golden and really crisp. Flip over and continue to cook for 5 minutes. Remove from the heat and allow to rest for a few minutes.

Split the brioche rolls in half and toast lightly under a hot grill. Stir the chives into the slaw, then divide between the rolls and top with a crispy chicken thigh. Sandwich with the top halves of the rolls and serve immediately with dill pickles if liked.

THE ULTIMATE

★

TURKEY CLUB

An American institution, found on menus from the very fanciest of hotels to the humble deli. Everyone has their own take on it, but these ingredients are consistent: sliced turkey or chicken, bacon, crisp lettuce and ripe tomato.

SERVES 4

TAKES 20 minutes

8 slices brown bread
4 slices white bread
4 tbsp good-quality mayonnaise
4 slices strong Cheddar cheese
4 slices hand-carved ham
3 small dill pickles, sliced
handful salad leaves
4 tsp American mustard
2 ripe, firm tomatoes, sliced
1 large ripe avocado, halved,
   stoned and peeled
300g (10oz) sliced cooked
   turkey breast
8 rashers cooked crispy bacon

Lightly toast the brown and white bread on both sides. Spread 4 slices of brown bread with a little mayo. Put a slice of cheese on each piece of bread, followed by a slice of ham and a few slices of pickle. Scatter a few salad leaves on top.

Spread one side of the 4 slices of white bread with the mustard and lay mustard-side down on the salad leaves. Brush the other side with a little more mayo, then add a layer of sliced tomatoes. Thinly slice the avocado and put on top of the tomato. Add a couple more salad leaves, then layer up with the turkey and finally 2 rashers of cooked bacon per sandwich.

Spread the remaining 4 slices of brown bread with mayo and use to enclose the sandwich, mayo side down. Secure with cocktail sticks and cut each sandwich into 4 triangles. Serve immediately.

CELEBRATION

★

TURKEY FEAST

Just too good to eat once or twice a year at Christmas
or Thanksgiving. You'll be making this chestnut,
apple and sage stuffing all year round to sandwich
with all of your cold cuts.

SERVES 6

TAKES 45 minutes

25g (scant 1oz) butter, plus extra
  for greasing
1 onion, finely chopped
1 eating apple, cored and
  finely chopped
3 tbsp dried cranberries
8 sage leaves, finely chopped
2 sprigs rosemary, leaves stripped
  and finely chopped
6 good-quality pork sausages
150g (5½oz) cooked, peeled
  chestnuts, roughly chopped
100g (3½oz) fresh breadcrumbs
salt and black pepper
12 slices crusty white bread
4 tbsp good-quality mayonnaise
300g (10oz) sliced turkey breast,
  or turkey leftovers
4–5 tbsp cranberry sauce

Heat the butter in a large, non-stick frying pan.
When bubbling, add the onion and cook for 5
minutes, or until starting to soften. Stir in the apple
and cranberries and cook for a further 2 minutes,
then remove from the heat, tip into a mixing bowl
and allow to cool.

Preheat the oven to 190°C/375°F fan/gas 5. Grease
and line a 20-cm (8-in) square tin with baking
parchment.

Add the sage and rosemary to the onion, then
squeeze the sausage meat from their skins into
the bowl. Add the chestnuts, breadcrumbs
and seasoning. Mix with your hands until fully
combined. Pack into the prepared baking tin and
bake for 30 minutes, or until golden and cooked
through. Remove from the oven and leave to stand
for 10 minutes.

Meanwhile, lay the bread slices on a board and
spread with the mayonnaise. Top half the bread
with turkey, then slice the stuffing and put on top,
followed by cranberry sauce. Sandwich with the
remaining bread slices and serve immediately.

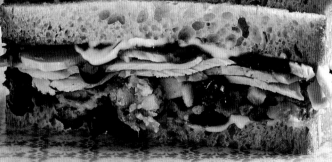

FRIED CHICKEN
★
WAFFLES

Crunchy, lightly spiced fried chicken sandwiched between fluffy waffles is a classic soul-food dish. If you're a fan of sweet and savoury you will love this combination – especially when doused generously in maple syrup.

SERVES 2

TAKES 20 minutes, plus marinating

200ml (7fl oz) buttermilk
4 boneless, skinless chicken thighs
salt and black pepper
100g (3½oz) plain (all-purpose) flour
50g (1¾oz) fine polenta (grits)
1 tsp smoked paprika
1 tsp garlic powder
¼ tsp cayenne pepper
500ml (17fl oz) vegetable oil
4 savoury waffles
maple syrup, to serve

Pour the buttermilk into a bowl, season the chicken thighs with salt, then submerge in the buttermilk and leave to stand for 15 minutes.

Tip the flour, polenta, paprika, garlic powder and cayenne into a baking dish. Season and stir to combine.

Pour the oil into a high-sided pan and heat to 160°C (320°F). Lift the chicken thighs out of the buttermilk, shaking off any excess, then plunge into the spiced flour mixture and turn until fully coated. The chicken will look a bit scabby and uneven – this is fine. Cook the chicken in batches (depending on the size of your pan) for 15 minutes, turning halfway through, until the chicken is cooked through and golden. Remove with a slotted spoon and drain on kitchen paper. Sprinkle with salt.

To serve, heat the waffles under a hot grill. Thickly slice the chicken and sandwich between two waffles, then drizzle with maple syrup.

CHICKEN & AVOCADO

★

CAESAR

If you have leftover chicken from a Sunday roast, this sandwich can be rustled up in a matter of minutes. The dressing can be made in advance and stored in the fridge for up to three days.

SERVES 4

TAKES 15 minutes

For the Caesar dressing
6 anchovy fillets in oil, drained and finely chopped
3 garlic cloves, crushed
4 tbsp good-quality mayonnaise
50g (1¾oz) Parmesan cheese, finely grated
2 tbsp olive oil
juice 1 lemon
salt and black pepper

8 slices crusty brown bread
2 cooked chicken breasts, sliced, or leftover roast chicken (see page 54)
1 large ripe avocado, halved, stoned and peeled
1 romaine lettuce, cut into roughly 5-cm (2-in) lengths

To make the dressing, mix the anchovies, garlic, mayo, Parmesan, oil and half the lemon juice in a bowl. Season with black pepper, but taste for salt as the anchovies will be salty.

Spread half the dressing over one side of each slice of bread. Slice the avocado and place the chicken and avocado slices over the base, then squeeze over the remaining lemon juice and season. Toss the lettuce with remaining dressing, then place over the avocado. Sandwich with the remaining bread slices and serve.

CHICKEN WITH
★
BRIE & ROASTED GRAPES

This sandwich is best served when the chicken and grapes are still warm. The juicy grapes pop in the mouth and act like chutney – they work so well with the crispy-skinned chicken and creamy brie.

SERVES 4

TAKES 1 hour

4 skin-on chicken thighs
3 garlic cloves, unpeeled
small handful thyme sprigs
2 tbsp extra virgin olive oil
salt and black pepper
300g (10½oz) seedless red grapes, pulled from the stalks
1 tbsp balsamic vinegar
½ tsp Dijon mustard
8 slices grainy brown bread
100g (3½oz) brie, sliced
couple handfuls lamb's lettuce, to serve

Preheat the oven to 200°C/400°F fan/gas 6.

Place the chicken, skin-side up, in a baking dish with the garlic and thyme. Toss with 1 tablespoon of the oil, season the chicken skin, then roast for 30 minutes. Ten minutes before the end of cooking, add the grapes and continue to cook.

Remove the tray from the oven and stir in the vinegar. Return to the oven and roast for a further 8 minutes, or until the meat is cooked through and the skin is golden and crisp. Transfer the chicken to a chopping board, allow to cool for 10 minutes, then slice.

Meanwhile, transfer the roasted grapes to a plate. In the tray, squash the garlic out of their skins (discarding the skins) and stir in the remaining oil, with the mustard and some seasoning. Mix with the tray juices to make a dressing. Spread half the dressing across four slices of bread, then layer with chicken, grapes, brie and a few leaves of lamb's lettuce. Drizzle over the remaining dressing, sandwich with the remaining bread slices and serve.

MEXICAN-STYLE
★
CHICKEN TORTAS

Tortas are loaded with many of the ingredients you'd expect to see piled inside a burrito or on a taco, but the soft toasty rolls make these ultimately more comforting and filling. This is definitely a hearty meal packed into a roll.

SERVES 4

TAKES 20 minutes

435g (15oz) cooked chicken thighs
2 tbsp olive oil
1 onion, finely sliced
1 red (bell) pepper, finely sliced
1 tsp ground cumin
1 tsp chilli powder
1 tsp smoked paprika
1 lime
salt and black pepper
435g (15oz) can refried beans
4 large, soft white rolls
100g (3½oz) strong Cheddar
   cheese, grated
1 large ripe avocado, halved,
   stoned and peeled
2–3 tbsp sliced jalapenos, drained

Discard the skin and bones from the chicken and shred the meat into bite-sized pieces. Set aside. Heat the oil in a large, non-stick frying pan. Fry the onion and red pepper for 5 minutes, or until starting to soften and take on some colour. Add the cumin, chilli and paprika, and cook for a further minute. Stir the chicken into the onion and pepper and coat in the spices. Halve the lime and squeeze in the juice of one half. Season and remove from the heat.

Meanwhile, heat the refried beans according to the instructions. Split the rolls in half, lay them on a baking sheet and toast under a hot grill on both sides until lightly golden. Spread the bottom halves with refried beans and sprinkle over the cheese. Scoop out and spoon over the avocado, pile on the chicken mixture and scatter over the jalapenos. Sandwich the two halves together and eat immediately. Serve with the remaining lime half cut into wedges for squeezing.

FISH

★

SANDWICHES

CLASSIC SMOKED SALMON &
CREAM CHEESE

It's always a tough decision choosing which bagel topping
to go for. Here is my posh take on the classic
New york city bagel.

SERVES 6

TAKES 15 minutes

180g (6oz) full-fat cream cheese
2 tbsp chopped chives
freshly ground black pepper
6 bagels
200g (7oz) smoked salmon
2 tbsp capers, drained
½ small red onion, thinly sliced
lemon wedges, to serve

Beat the cream cheese until it is soft and
spreadable. Stir in the chives and plenty of
black pepper.

Split the bagels in half and toast under a hot grill
until golden. Spread each cut side with the cream
cheese. Layer over the smoked salmon, transfer
to a platter and sprinkle over the capers and red
onions. Serve with lemon wedges.

Pictured on page 78 (top)

BEETROOT, HORSERADISH &
★
MACKEREL

An homage to the Scandinavian open sandwich, this bagel
is the perfect way to accompany all things *hygge*. Use
smoked mackerel to add punch to your brunch.

SERVES 6

TAKES 15 minutes

250g (9oz) cooked beetroots
(beets), drained
2 tbsp good-quality mayonnaise
2 tbsp horseradish cream
2 tbsp chopped dill
salt and black pepper
6 seeded bagels
225g (8oz) peppered smoked
mackerel

Finely dice the beetroots into small cubes. Transfer
to a bowl and add the mayo, horseradish and most
of the dill. Stir and season.

Split the bagels in half and toast under a hot grill
until golden. Spoon the beetroot salad over each
cut side. Flake the smoked mackerel over the top
and serve sprinkled with the reserved dill.

Pictured on page 78 (left)

SPRING ONION &

★

HADDOCK SALAD

Complete your bagel brunch with this fresh and filling
sandwich. You can use any white fish here, but
good-quality haddock and crisp spring onions
are a match made in fishy heaven.

SERVES 6

TAKES 25 minutes

300g (10½oz) undyed, skinless,
  boneless haddock fillets
3 tbsp good-quality mayonnaise
1 tsp Dijon mustard
4 spring onions (scallions),
  chopped
1 lemon
salt and black pepper
6 bagels

Put the fish in a shallow microwavable dish. Add 2
tablespoons of water, cover with plastic wrap and
microwave for 1½–3 minutes. If you don't have
a microwave, put the fish in a shallow pan, with
just enough water to cover, and cook gently until
opaque and cooked through. Drain and allow to
cool completely.

Flake the fish into a bowl and add the mayo,
mustard and spring onions. Zest the lemon and add
it to the fish mixture along with a squeeze of juice,
stir and season. Add more lemon if it needs it. Split
the bagels in half and toast under a hot grill until
golden. Spread the white fish salad on the cut sides
and serve straight away.

Pictured on page 79

REMOULADE &
★
PRAWN PO'BOY

The po'boy, or 'poor boy', harks from New Orleans, where flavour is king and fresh, fried fish is everywhere.

SERVES 2

TAKES 30 minutes

For the remoulade sauce
3 tbsp good-quality mayonnaise
2 tsp wholegrain mustard
¼ tsp hot sauce, plus extra to serve
¼ tsp paprika
1 tsp capers, finely chopped
1 spring onion (scallion), finely
    chopped
salt and black pepper

50g (1¾oz) plain (all-purpose) flour
75g (2½oz) fine polenta (grits)
1 tsp cayenne pepper
1 tsp garlic powder
1 tsp paprika
½ tsp celery salt
salt and black pepper
1 medium egg
500ml (17fl oz) vegetable oil
150g (5½oz) raw king prawns
    (shrimps)

Start by making the remoulade sauce. In a small bowl, mix the mayo, mustard, hot sauce, paprika, capers and spring onion together. Season well and set aside.

Mix the flour, polenta and spices in a baking dish and season. Crack the egg into a separate bowl and whisk with a fork.

Heat the oil in a high-sided pan over a medium–high heat. Dip the prawns in the flour mixture, coating fully and shaking off any excess. Dip immediately into the beaten egg, again shaking off any excess, then plunge back into the seasoned flour.

Test whether the oil is hot enough by dropping in a cube of bread – it should bubble and turn golden in about 30 seconds. Carefully lower the prawns into the hot oil and cook in batches, being careful

ingredients and method continue overleaf...

★ ★ ★ ★ ★ ★ ★ ★ ★ ★ ★ ★ ★ ★ ★

★ ★

PRAWN PO' BOY

continued...

2 sub rolls or soft baguettes
¼ iceberg lettuce, shredded
2 ripe tomatoes, sliced
lemon wedges, to serve

not to overcrowd the pan. When the prawns float to the surface (they will take 2–3 minutes), scoop them out with a slotted spoon, drain on kitchen paper and sprinkle with salt.

To serve, split the rolls in half lengthways. Spread the cut sides with remoulade sauce, add some lettuce and tomatoes, then pile with crispy fried prawns. Serve with lemon wedges for squeezing and extra hot sauce, if liked.

TARTARE SAUCE &

★

FISH FINGERS

When you're hungry and pushed for time there is
nothing better than a fish finger butty. Keep a stash of fish
fingers in your freezer for a quick dinner, lunch
or the perfect hangover cure.

SERVES 2

TAKES 15 minutes

6 large or 8 small fish fingers
For the tartare sauce
2 heaped tbsp good-quality
  mayonnaise
½ shallot, finely chopped
1 dill pickle, finely chopped
1 tbsp capers, drained
few sprigs of dill, roughly chopped

4 thick slices white bread
¼ iceberg lettuce, shredded

Cook the fish fingers according to packet
instructions.

Mix the mayo, shallot, pickle, capers and dill
together. Lay the bread on a board and spread each
slice with the tartare sauce. Pile the lettuce on
two pieces, top with the cooked fish fingers, then
sandwich the two slices together and devour.

AVOCADO WITH
★
PRAWN COCKTAIL

A retro classic brought up to date with a kick of chilli heat
and slices of creamy avocado. Any table looks posher
with a platter of prawn sandwiches.

SERVES 4

TAKES 15 minutes

3 tbsp good-quality mayonnaise
1 tbsp tomato ketchup
1 tbsp Sriracha chilli sauce
300g (10½oz) cooked and peeled
    North Atlantic prawns (shrimps)
salt and black pepper
8 slices wholegrain brown bread
¼ iceberg lettuce, shredded
1 spring onion (scallion),
    thinly sliced
1 ripe avocado, peeled and stoned

In a bowl, mix the mayo, ketchup and chilli sauce to
make a cocktail sauce. Drain the prawns to remove
any excess liquid. Toss with the sauce, season and
set aside.

Lay four slices of bread on a board and divide the
prawn cocktail between the slices. Scatter over the
lettuce and spring onion. Thinly slice the avocado
and lay on top of the lettuce. Sandwich with the
top half of the bread, cut into triangles and serve
immediately.

LOBSTER

★

ROLLS

Traditional lobster rolls are buttery and crisp at the edges
and pillowy-soft in the centre. Lobster is a real treat but
you could also try this recipe with some chopped-up,
cooked king prawns instead.

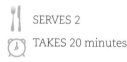

SERVES 2

TAKES 20 minutes

1 cooked lobster
1 celery stick, finely chopped
1 spring onion (scallion),
   finely chopped
1 tbsp chopped chives
2–3 tbsp good-quality mayonnaise
½ lemon
salt and black pepper
2–4 brioche hotdog rolls
   (depending on their size)
1 tbsp softened butter

Gently crack your lobster with a rolling pin and
remove the meat from the tail-end. Pull out the
claw meat and the meat inside the knuckles, then
discard the shell. Cut the lobster meat into bite-
sized pieces and transfer to a bowl.

Add the celery and spring onion to the lobster
along with the chives, mayo and a good squeeze
of lemon juice. Taste and season with a little salt
and plenty of black pepper. Set aside.

Spread the outsides of the brioche rolls with
butter. Heat a large, non-stick frying pan over
a medium–high heat and fry the rolls all over
for 1–2 minutes, until golden and crisp.

Remove from the pan, split the rolls down the
middle and pile in the lobster mixture. Serve
immediately with plenty of napkins.

PINK ONIONS &
★
PICKLED HERRING

You can make all the components of these open sandwiches in advance and assemble just before serving.

🍴 SERVES 4

⏰ TAKES 15 minutes

1 small red onion, finely sliced
juice ½ lemon
¼ tsp caster (superfine) sugar
4 heaped tbsp crème fraîche
handful chives
handful dill, finely chopped, plus
   a few fronds for garnish
salt and black pepper
¼ small red cabbage, finely
   shredded
4 large slices dark rye bread
240g (9oz) pickled herring,
   drained and chopped

Put the onion in a small bowl with the lemon juice and stir in the sugar. Cover and set aside.

In a separate bowl, mix the crème fraîche with the herbs and plenty of seasoning.

Add the cabbage to a third bowl and pour over a little of the liquid from the pickled onion, along with a good pinch of salt. Toss to coat and leave to stand for a few minutes.

Meanwhile, lightly toast the rye bread on both sides, then spread with the herby crème fraîche. Lift the cabbage out of the bowl, shaking to remove any excess liquid. Pile on top of the crème fraîche, followed by the pickled herring. Remove the onion with a slotted spoon and scatter over the top of the herring along with a few dill fronds. Eat immediately.

PICKLED CUCUMBER &
★
SMOKED TROUT

These rolls make for a sophisticated light lunch. You could make double the dill mustard dressing and keep it in the fridge to dress any salad leaves before serving.

SERVES 4

TAKES 15 minutes

For the dill mustard dressing
3 tbsp light olive oil
1½ tbsp white wine vinegar,
   plus a drizzle
1 tbsp Dijon mustard
¼ tsp caster (superfine) sugar
handful dill, finely chopped
salt and black pepper
For the cucumber salad
2 small cucumbers, thinly sliced
1 dill pickle, thinly sliced
1 shallot, thinly sliced

4 brown bread rolls
4 tbsp cream cheese
250g (9oz) hot-smoked trout

Start by making the dressing. In a small bowl, whisk the oil, vinegar, mustard and sugar until combined and emulsified – the dressing should look yellow and creamy. Stir in most of the dill, reserving some for sprinkling, and season.

To make the salad, tip the cucumbers, dill pickle and shallot into the bowl with the dressing and leave to stand for 5 minutes.

Cut the rolls in half. Lightly toast the cut sides of the rolls under a hot grill. Remove and spread each bottom half with 1 tablespoon of cream cheese. Flake over the trout, then spoon over the cucumber salad and any dressing. Sprinkle with the reserved dill, sandwich with the top of the rolls and serve immediately.

THE ULTIMATE
★
TUNA MAYO

Forget those bland tuna sandwiches of old. These are the
ultimate tuna sarnies, packed full of big flavours and bold
colours. A feast for the eyes and the belly.

SERVES 4

TAKES 20 minutes

3 medium eggs
2 x 200-g (7-oz) cans tuna
   in oil, drained
4 tbsp good-quality mayonnaise
1 tbsp Dijon mustard
salt and black pepper
6 cornichons, finely chopped
½ red onion, finely chopped
2 cooked beetroots (beets),
   finely chopped
1 large crusty ciabatta loaf
100g (3½oz) watercress, or other
   salad leaves

Cook the eggs in a pan of boiling water for 8
minutes. Drain and run under cold water until
completely cool, then peel and set aside.

Flake the tuna into a bowl and add 3 tablespoons
of the mayo, the mustard, a little salt and plenty of
black pepper. Stir in the cornichons and red onion,
then gently fold through the beetroot – you want
a light mottled pink mixture.

Split the ciabatta loaf in half lengthways and spread
with the remaining mayo on both sides. Thinly slice
the hard-boiled eggs and lay on the bottom layer.
Top with a generous layer of tuna, followed by
handfuls of green leaves. Cut into thick slices
and serve.

PROVENÇAL

★

PAN BAGNAT

The perfect food to pack up for a seaside picnic, this sandwich really benefits from sitting around for an hour or so to allow all of the classic niçoise flavours to meld and the bread to soak up the juices.

SERVES 4

TAKES 20 minutes, plus standing

4 medium eggs
6 baby potatoes
6 anchovy fillets, finely chopped
2 tbsp capers, roughly chopped
1 garlic clove, crushed
1 tbsp Dijon mustard
3 tbsp olive oil
2 tbsp red wine vinegar
1 shallot, finely chopped
200g (7oz) mixed pitted olives,
   roughly chopped
cracked black pepper
2 large ciabatta loaves
large handful parsley, chopped
2 red (bell) peppers from a jar,
   drained and sliced
2 x 200-g (7-oz) cans tuna fish
   in oil, drained
2 large ripe tomatoes, sliced

Cook the eggs and potatoes in a large pan of boiling, salted water for 9 minutes. Check the potatoes – they should be tender. If they are still hard, remove the eggs and carry on cooking the potatoes until easily pierced with a sharp knife. Drain and run under cold running water to cool. Drain again, then peel the eggs. Thinly slice the potatoes and the eggs. Set aside.

In a bowl, mix the anchovies, capers, garlic and mustard. Whisk in the oil and vinegar. Fold in the shallot and olives, and season with black pepper.

Split the ciabatta loaves in half lengthways. Stir the parsley into the anchovy mixture, then spread most of it over the cut sides of the bread. Arrange the sliced eggs and potatoes over one side, followed by the red peppers, then drizzle over a little of the remaining dressing. Flake the tuna onto the other side of the bread and drizzle with the remaining dressing. Lay the tomatoes on top. Carefully sandwich the two halves together and wrap tightly in plastic wrap. Leave to stand at room temperature for 1 hour, or chill until ready to slice and serve.

CRAB

★

MIMOSA

Possibly the poshest of all the seafood salads, traditionally delicately layered up in a bowl and adorned with finely chopped egg whites and sieved yolks. The yolk is said to emulate the pretty flowers of the mimosa tree.

SERVES 4

TAKES 20 minutes

2 medium eggs
2 tbsp good-quality mayonnaise
1 tsp Dijon mustard
1 spring onion (scallion),
   finely chopped
pinch paprika
4 slices buttery brioche bread
1 small ripe avocado, halved,
   stoned and peeled
1 tomato, deseeded and finely
   chopped
150g (5½oz) white crab meat (use
   white and brown if you prefer)

Cook the eggs in a pan of boiling water for 8 minutes, then run under cold water until completely cool. Drain, peel and halve the eggs. Carefully scoop out the yolks, leaving no traces of yellow in the white. Push the yolks through a sieve or finely chop and collect in a small bowl. Finely chop the whites and set aside in a separate bowl.

Mix the mayo, mustard, spring onion and paprika together. Lightly toast the bread on both sides under a hot grill, then spread with the mayo mixture. Finely slice the avocado and fan it over the bread. Scatter with tomato, then flake over the crab meat and egg whites. Finally, finish with the sieved egg yolks. Serve immediately.

MADRID-STYLE CRISPY
★
SQUID ROLLS

You can't visit Madrid without devouring a crusty white roll stuffed with freshly fried calamari. This recipe is made a little bit posher with the addition of yet more Spanish flavours – a smoky aïoli and deep-fried garlic and chilli.

 SERVES 4

 TAKES 30 minutes

For the smoky aïoli
5 tbsp good-quality mayonnaise
1 tsp smoked, sweet paprika
1 small garlic clove, crushed
salt and black pepper

500g (1lb 2oz) squid (get your
    fishmonger to gut and clean
    it for you)
100g (3½oz) cornflour (cornstarch)
100g (3½oz) plain (all-purpose)
    flour
1 litre (1¾ pints) vegetable oil
2 red chillies, thinly sliced on
    the diagonal
2 large garlic cloves, thinly sliced

4 crusty white rolls
lemon wedges, to serve

Start by making the smoky aïoli. In a bowl, mix the mayo, paprika and garlic together. Season, then cover and set aside.

Cut the squid into 5-mm rings. In a baking dish, mix the flours with plenty of seasoning. Heat the oil to 180°C (355°F) in a high-sided pan over a medium–high heat, or test with a cube of bread (it should bubble and turn golden in 20 seconds). Tip the squid into the seasoned flour and toss to completely coat. Fry in batches until crisp and floating to the surface. Remove with a slotted spoon, drain on kitchen paper and sprinkle with salt.

Fry the chillies and garlic in the hot oil for about 1 minute, or until golden and softened. Remove with a slotted spoon and scatter over the squid.

Split the bread rolls in half and spread with smoky aïoli. Divide the squid, chillies and garlic between the rolls and serve with lemon wedges alongside for squeezing.

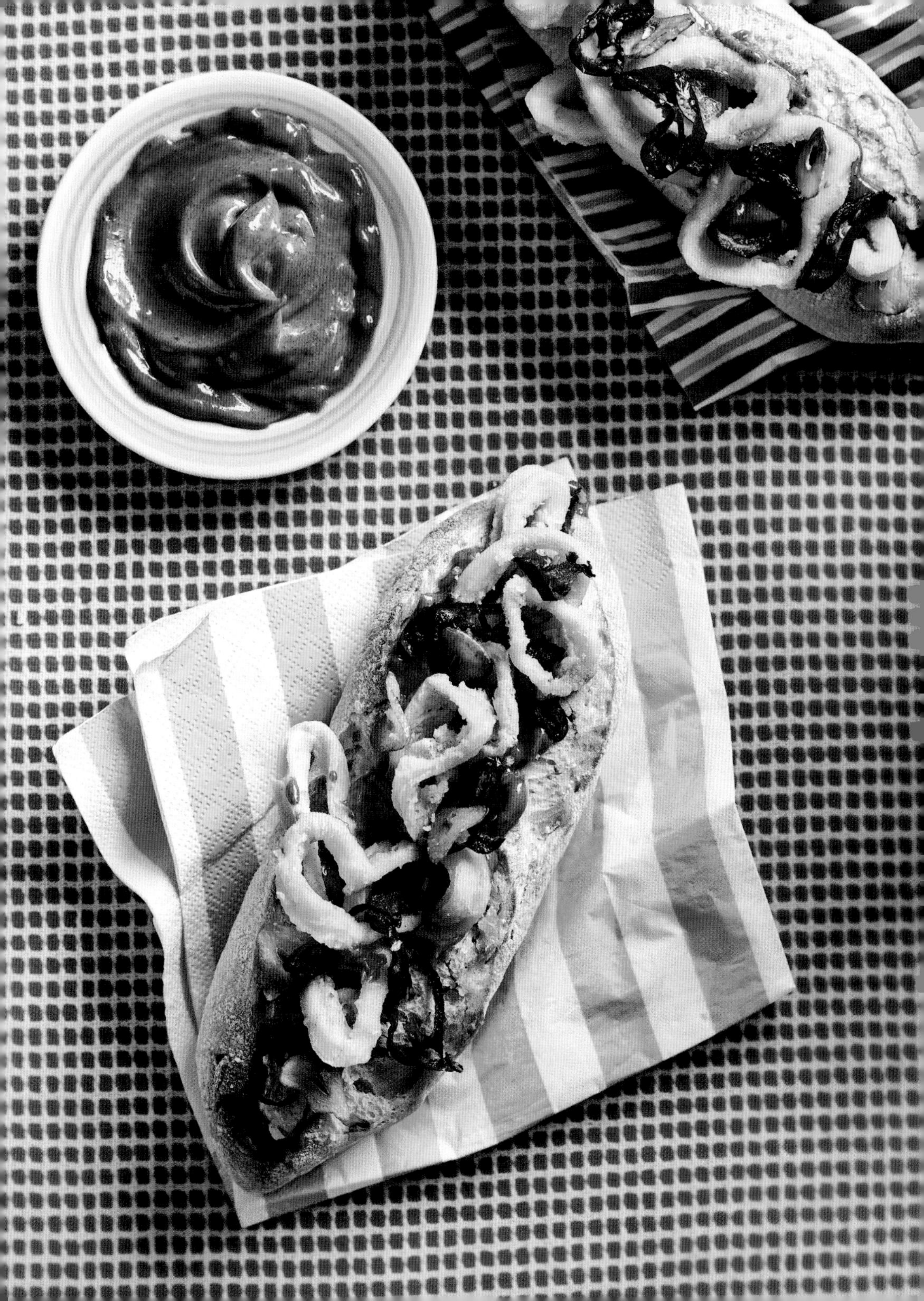

VEGETARIAN

★

SANDWICHES

CLASSIC

★

HUMMUS

This classic Middle-Eastern dip is incredibly easy to make.
Keep a pot of hummus in the fridge at all times – it will
make almost every sandwich posher!

SERVES 4

TAKES 15 minutes

1 tsp cumin seeds
1 tsp salt
660g (1lb 7oz) jar chickpeas
   (or 2 x 400-g [14-oz] cans)
1 small garlic clove, crushed
juice 1 lemon
3 tbsp tahini
3 tbsp olive oil

Toast the cumin seeds in a frying pan until fragrant.
Tip out into a pestle and mortar, add the salt and
grind to a fine powder.

Drain the chickpeas, reserving the liquid from
the jar. Tip the chickpeas into the bowl of a food
processor, add the cumin powder and garlic.
Squeeze in the lemon juice, add the tahini, olive oil
and about 3 tablespoons of the liquid from the jar.
Pulse until completely smooth. You may have to
remove the bowl and scrape down the sides with
a spatula to get the hummus going, but resist the
urge to add too much of the liquid as it will make
the hummus too thin.

Cover and chill until required.

Pictured on page 104 (top left)

HUMMUS, AUBERGINE &
★
BOILED EGG PITTAS

Best friends with hummus, the pitta is the perfect pocket
for stuffing full of all your favourite foods.
Great for a posh lunch on the go.

SERVES 4

TAKES 20 minutes

1 quantity Classic Hummus
   (opposite)
4 eggs
2 tbsp olive oil
1 aubergine (eggplant), chopped
   into 1.5-cm (½-in) dice
salt and black pepper
4 pitta breads
handful flat-leaf parsley leaves
cucumber spears and pickles,
   to serve

Cook the eggs in a pan of boiling water for
8 minutes, then run under cold water until
completely cool. Set aside.

Heat the oil in a large frying pan over a high heat
and fry the aubergine cubes for 8–10 minutes,
stirring frequently, until golden and soft. Remove
from heat and season.

Quarter the eggs, toast the pitta breads and
split. Fill with hummus, egg and fried aubergine
and sprinkle with the parsley leaves. Serve with
cucumber spears and pickles alongside.

Pictured on page 104 (top)

ZESTY GREENS

Crisp carrot and zesty greens are a great match with creamy
home-made hummus. A sandwich that's easy
to prepare but packs a veggie punch.

SERVES 4

TAKES 15 minutes

½ orange
1 tbsp clear honey
2 tsp Dijon mustard
2 tbsp olive oil
salt and black pepper
100g (3½oz) spinach, watercress
  and rocket (arugula) salad
1 quantity Classic Hummus
  (page 106)
8 slices granary bread
1 large carrot, coarsely grated

Zest the orange and squeeze the juice into a large
bowl. Add the honey, mustard and oil, and whisk
until combined and emulsified. Season, then tip in
the green leaves and toss to coat in the dressing.

Spread each slice of bread with hummus, scatter
four slices with carrot and divide the green leaves
over the top. Sandwich with the remaining slices of
bread and cut into triangles before serving.

Pictured on page 104 (bottom)

HUMMUS, TOMATO &
★
GARLIC BEANS

This is an open sandwich for garlic lovers everywhere.
Simple to make but delicious – add an extra drizzle
of olive oil at the end for ultimate indulgence.

SERVES 4

TAKES 30 minutes

200g (7oz) fine green beans
2 tbsp olive oil
2 garlic cloves, finely chopped
100g (3½oz) cherry tomatoes,
 halved
salt and black pepper
4 large slices crusty bread
1 quantity Classic Hummus
 (page 106)

Cook the green beans in a large pan of boiling,
salted water for 4 minutes, then run under cold
water until cool. Drain and set aside.

Heat the oil in a large non-stick frying pan over a
medium–high heat. Add the garlic and sizzle for a
few seconds until fragrant, then throw in the green
beans and toss to coat in the garlic. Turn up the
heat to high and add the tomatoes with plenty of
seasoning, shaking the pan for 2–3 minutes, until
the tomatoes begin to break down.

Lightly toast the bread on both sides, spread with
hummus and pile with garlicky beans and tomatoes.
Serve immediately.

Pictured on page 105 (bottom)

TWICE-FRIED HAND-CUT
★
CHIP BUTTIES

If you are not familiar with the joys of a chip butty, then you really must try this recipe. You have to be generous with the butter, the salt and of course the chips. Best served with a piping-hot mug of tea and ketchup, if you like.

 SERVES 4

TAKES 35 minutes, plus cooling

8 slices thick-cut white bread
softened butter, for spreading
1kg (2lb 4oz) potatoes (I used
   Maris Piper)
1 litre vegetable oil, for deep frying
sea salt flakes
tomato ketchup, to serve
   (optional)

Spread one side of each slice of bread generously with butter.

Line a couple of baking sheets with kitchen paper. Peel and cut the potatoes into thick finger-sized chips, about 6 x 1.5cm (2¼ x ½in). Place in a bowl of cold water as you go. Drain well. Cook the potatoes in a large pan of boiling, salted water for 5–8 minutes, or until just tender. Drain really well, then spread out on the prepared sheets to thoroughly dry and cool.

Pour the oil into a medium saucepan and heat to 140°C (285°F) – a cooking thermometer will help you achieve an accurate temperature. Cook the potatoes in batches for 6–8 minutes until they start to take on some colour. Remove with a slotted spoon and drain on more kitchen paper while you cook the remaining potatoes.

Increase the temperature of the oil to 190°C (375°F) and cook the chips in batches for a second time for 2–3 minutes, or until golden-brown, crisp on the outside and fluffy in the middle. Remove from the oil with a slotted spoon, drain on kitchen paper, season with salt and serve immediately stuffed between two slices of thickly buttered bread.

ROASTED GARLIC AÏOLI WITH
★
CAULIFLOWER

Cauliflower steaks are a great veggie sandwich filler.
Charred at the edges and soft in the centre, they give the
meaty variety a run for their money.

SERVES 4

TAKES 45 minutes

1 large or 2 small cauliflowers
4 tbsp olive oil, plus extra for
   greasing
1 tbsp smoked paprika
1 tsp ground cumin
½ tsp chilli flakes
salt and black pepper
3 fat garlic cloves, unpeeled
2 red onions, cut into wedges
5 tbsp good-quality mayonnaise
½ lemon

4 large crusty rolls
60g (2oz) rocket (arugula)
handful shop-bought crispy
   shallots

Preheat the oven to 200°C/400°F/gas 6.

Discard the cauliflower leaves and cut it horizontally
into four thick steaks. Lightly grease a baking dish
with oil and lay the cauli steaks on top. Mix the
spices together with plenty of seasoning, then stir
in 3 tablespoons of the oil. Pour over the steaks and
use your hands to coat both sides. Add the garlic.

Roast for 10 minutes. Pick out and reserve the
garlic, toss in the onion wedges and the remaining
oil and return to the oven for 35 minutes, turning
the steaks a couple of times. The steaks should be
tender in the middle and golden on the outside.

To make the roasted garlic aïoli, squeeze the soft
flesh from the papery garlic skins into a bowl and
stir in the mayo. Season and set aside. Squeeze the
lemon juice over the cauli steaks and onions, and
gently toss the onions to coat.

Halve the rolls and chargrill, cut-side down, for a
few minutes. Spread the cut sides with the aïoli. Put
a handful of rocket and a cauli steak on the bottom
half, followed by a spoonful of roasted onions and
some crispy shallots for crunch. Sandwich with the
tops and serve immediately.

ROMESCO WITH
★
SPANISH OMELETTE

Spanish omelettes are perfect for using up any leftover ingredients you might have lingering in the fridge. Feel free to experiment and add anything you like – chorizo works brilliantly for non-veggie pals.

SERVES 4–6

TAKES 1 hour

650g (1lb 7oz) waxy potatoes
2 tbsp olive oil, plus extra
    for drizzling
large knob butter
2 onions, finely sliced
8 large eggs
100g (3½oz) Manchego cheese
salt and black pepper
handful parsley, chopped
3 ripe tomatoes, halved
For the romesco sauce
3½ tbsp olive oil
50g (1¾oz) roasted almonds
3 roasted peppers from a jar,
    drained and roughly chopped
1 tbsp red wine vinegar
1 tbsp sweet smoked paprika
½ garlic clove, crushed

6 crusty rolls
100g (3½oz) rocket (arugula)

Cut the potatoes into 5-mm slices. Cook in a pan of boiling, salted water for 8 minutes, or until just tender. Drain really well and allow to steam dry. Heat the oil and butter in a large frying pan over a medium heat, then fry the onions for 10 minutes until starting to soften and turn golden. Tip in the potatoes and stir to coat with the onions. Remove from the heat and allow to cool slightly.

Preheat the oven to 180°C/350°F/gas 4. Line a high-sided baking dish with baking parchment. In a jug, beat together the eggs, grate in half the cheese and season well. Spread the potatoes and onions over the baking sheet, scatter with parsley, then pour the egg mixture over the top. Bake for 20–25 minutes, or until set and lightly golden. Put the tomatoes on a baking sheet, drizzle with a little oil, season and roast for 15 minutes.

Put all the ingredients for the romesco sauce into a food processor and blend until smooth. To serve, split the rolls, drizzle the cut sides with oil and griddle for a few minutes. Spread with the romesco sauce. Cut the omelette into squares and pop into each sandwich. Shave the remaining Manchego over the top, add a tomato half, some rocket and the top halves of the buns.

KIMCHI

★

GRILLED CHEESE

Spreading the outside of the bread with mayo instead of butter means that you get an even, golden crispy outside to your oozy grilled-cheese sandwiches. The combination of melted cheese and crisp spicy kimchi is unbeatable.

SERVES 2

TAKES 15 minutes

125g (4½oz) strong Cheddar cheese
75g (2½oz) kimchi, shredded, plus extra to serve
2 spring onions (scallions), finely sliced
4 thick slices sourdough bread
2 tbsp good-quality mayonnaise

Coarsely grate the cheese into a bowl, stir in the kimchi and spring onions, and set aside.

Spread the bread with mayo on one side. Heat a large, non-stick frying pan over a medium heat. Put two slices of bread, mayo-side down, into the pan. Top each slice of bread with the cheese mixture. Top with the other slices of bread, mayo side-up.

Cook for 2–3 minutes until crisp and golden, carefully flip over and cook on the other side until the cheese is melted. Remove from the pan and serve immediately with extra kimchi on the side.

SQUASH, COURGETTE &
★
MINTY FETA

Roasting the squash with fragrant spices like cinnamon heightens its natural sweetness, which makes it a perfect match for the cool, salty feta and yogurt sauce. If you fancy a lighter sandwich, pack the ingredients into a pitta.

SERVES 4

TAKES 1 hour

1 butternut squash
2 tbsp olive oil, plus a glug
4 garlic cloves, unpeeled
1 tsp chilli flakes
1 tsp ground cinnamon
1 tsp sweet smoked paprika
salt and black pepper
2 courgettes (zucchinis), cut into
    5mm slices lengthways
200g (7oz) feta cheese
100g (3½oz) thick Greek yogurt
handful mint, finely chopped
8 slices crusty granary bread
handful pitted Kalamata
    olives, roughly chopped

Preheat the oven to 190°C/375°F/gas 5.

Halve the squash lengthways, scoop out the seeds and cut into 1-cm (⅜-in) thick slices, then tip into a roasting tray and toss with the oil, garlic, chilli, cinnamon, paprika and seasoning. Roast for 45 minutes, picking out and reserving the garlic halfway through cooking. Gently stir the squash and continue to cook until soft and caramelised.

Meanwhile, heat a griddle pan to high. Brush the courgettes with a little oil, then cook for 3–5 minutes, turning halfway through, or until charred and starting to soften. Remove and set aside.

Squeeze the garlic out of their skins, add to a bowl and mash with a fork. Crumble in the feta and yogurt. Stir to combine, season, then add most of the mint. Set aside.

To assemble the sandwiches, spread the bread with equal amounts of the feta mixture. Divide the courgette and squash between four slices and dot over the olives and the reserved mint. Sandwich with the remaining four slices and serve.

MUSHROOMS, STICKY ONIONS & BLUE CHEESE

This sandwich definitely won't leave your vegetarian friends feeling short-changed. The flavours work so well and meld together to give an earthy, soft, sweet and savoury delicious, melty mess of a sandwich.

SERVES 2

TAKES 25 minutes

25g (scant 1oz) butter
4 small onions, finely sliced
2 sprigs thyme, leaves picked
1 tbsp balsamic vinegar
1 tsp sugar
salt and black pepper
4 portobello mushrooms
100g (3½oz) blue cheese
2 ciabatta rolls
1 tbsp good-quality mayonnaise
1 tsp Dijon mustard
handful watercress

Heat the butter in a large, non-stick frying pan. Add the onions and thyme and fry for 15–20 minutes, stirring occasionally, until soft and golden. Pour in the vinegar and add the sugar with plenty of seasoning. Stir for a further minute to dissolve the sugar, then remove from the heat.

Meanwhile, clean off any dirt from the mushrooms. Remove the stalks and discard. Heat a griddle pan to high. Place the mushrooms gill-side down and cook for 3 minutes. Flip the mushrooms over and cook for 2 minutes, tipping out any water that accumulates inside the mushroom cup. Fill each cup with blue cheese and cook for a further 2 minutes until the mushrooms are soft and the cheese is molten.

Split the rolls in half and toast or griddle. Mix the mayo and mustard together and spread on the base of each roll. Add some watercress, then top each with two cheese-filled mushrooms and a generous scoop of sticky onions. Serve immediately with lots of black pepper.

AUBERGINE
★
PARMIGIANA

Traditional *melanzane alla parmigiana* is made by layering up fried aubergine slices with a rich tomato sauce, mozzarella and Parmesan. It's gooey, savoury and deeply moreish. This is all that, but in a sandwich.

SERVES 4

TAKES 45 minutes

For the tomato sauce
1 tbsp olive oil
1 onion, finely chopped
2 garlic cloves, finely chopped
1 tsp dried oregano
400-g (14-oz) can chopped
    tomatoes
pinch sugar
salt and black pepper

1 large aubergine (eggplant),
    sliced lengthways into
    ¾-cm (¼-in) slices
3 tbsp olive oil
4 ciabatta rolls
75g (2½oz) Parmesan
    cheese, grated
150g (5½oz) ball mozzarella
    cheese, drained and sliced

Start by making the tomato sauce. Heat the oil in a large saucepan. Fry the onion for 5 minutes, or until starting to soften and take on some colour. Add the garlic and fry for 1 minute until fragrant. Tip in the oregano and tomatoes and simmer for 15 minutes, or until the sauce has thickened slightly. Stir in the sugar and season to taste.

Heat a griddle pan or grill to high. Brush the aubergine slices with the oil and cook for 2–3 minutes on each side until charred and softened. You might have to do this in batches, keeping any cooked aubergines in a warm oven.

Preheat the oven to 200°C/400°F /gas 6. Split the ciabatta rolls in half, spooning tomato sauce over the cut sides. Sprinkle with the Parmesan, then layer the griddled aubergine over one half followed by the mozzarella. Sandwich with the top half and return to the oven for 8–10 minutes for the cheese to melt and all the flavours to meld together.

GREEN GODDESS SAUCE WITH
HALLOUMI

Green goddess sauce, given a creamy addition
with ripe avocado, complements the salty,
slightly sharp halloumi wonderfully.

SERVES 4

TAKES 20 minutes

For the green goddess sauce
1 ripe avocado, stoned and peeled
juice ½ lemon
2 tbsp Greek yogurt
1 mild green chilli, roughly
    chopped
½ garlic clove, crushed
handful coriander (cilantro)
salt and black pepper

250g (9oz) block halloumi cheese
8 baby plum tomatoes
olive oil
8 slices sourdough bread

Start by making the green goddess sauce. Roughly
chop the avocado and put it into the bowl of a
food processor with the lemon juice, yogurt, chilli
and garlic. Roughly chop most of the coriander and
add it to the bowl, reserving a few leaves. Season
and pulse until almost smooth. Cover and set aside.

Heat a griddle pan to high. Cut the halloumi into
eight slices and cook for 5 minutes, turning halfway
through until charred and soft. Add the tomatoes
to the pan. Griddle the tomatoes for 2–3 minutes
– you just want them to begin to soften and the
skins to pop. Remove, halve the tomatoes and
season with a little salt and a drizzle of oil.

Griddle the bread on both sides until warm and
lightly toasted. Spread four slices with green
goddess sauce, then lay a couple of slices of
halloumi and some tomato halves on top. Finish
with a sprinkle of the reserved coriander leaves
and sandwich with the remaining bread.

BEETROOT & GOAT'S CHEESE
★
CROQUE-MADAME

Traditional ham is replaced here with thinly sliced, smoky spiced beetroot. The earthy beets and goat's cheese stand up to the rich béchamel and add a welcome bite to the much-loved goo-fest that is a croque-madame.

SERVES 4

TAKES 45 minutes

8 small or 4 large beetroots (beets), scrubbed and thinly sliced
2 tbsp olive oil
1 tbsp smoked paprika
1 tsp chilli flakes
1 tbsp red wine vinegar
For the béchamel
25g (scant 1oz) butter
25g (scant 1oz) plain (all-purpose) flour
150ml (5¼fl oz) milk
1 tbsp Dijon mustard
150g (5½oz) Gruyère cheese, grated
salt and black pepper

8 slices good white bread, such as sourdough
125g (4½oz) soft goat's cheese
4 eggs

Preheat the oven to 200°C/400°F fan/gas 6. Spread the beetroots out on a baking sheet and toss with half of the oil, the smoked paprika and chilli flakes. Roast for 25 minutes, adding the vinegar after 15 minutes, and giving them a stir. Continue to cook until the beets are tender but still have a little bite.

Meanwhile, make the béchamel. Put the butter, flour and milk in a small saucepan over a medium heat and stir continuously until you have a smooth, thick white sauce – it should take 4–5 minutes. Stir in the mustard, half the Gruyère and plenty of seasoning. Remove from the heat and set aside.

Lightly toast the bread. Spread 4 slices with half the béchamel sauce, dot over the goat's cheese equally, then lay slices of beetroot on top. Sprinkle with a little Gruyère, saving some for the tops. Sandwich with the remaining slice of toasted bread. Heat a grill to medium. Transfer the sandwiches to a baking sheet and spread the remaining béchamel over the tops. Sprinkle with the reserved Gruyère and grill for 2–3 minutes, until bubbling and golden.

Heat the remaining oil in a frying pan and fry the eggs to your liking. Slide a fried egg on top of each croque-madame and serve immediately.

PICO DE GALLO &
★
SPICY BEAN QUESADILLAS

Quesadillas are so easy to make and versatile to boot. You can add anything into these Mexican-style sandwiches, from leftover roast meat to canned fish. For best results, always add plenty of cheese.

SERVES 4

TAKES 30 minutes

For the pico de gallo
1 small onion, finely chopped
2 large tomatoes, deseeded and
  finely chopped
handful coriander (cilantro),
  chopped
salt and black pepper

2 tbsp olive oil, plus a drizzle
1 onion, chopped
1 garlic clove, chopped
1 red chilli, chopped
2 tsp ground cumin
400g (14oz) can borlotti beans,
  rinsed and drained
400g (14oz) can black beans,
  rinsed and drained
8 corn tortillas
150g (5½oz) mature Cheddar
  cheese, coarsely grated

soured cream and hot sauce,
  to serve

Start by making the pico de gallo. Mix all the ingredients in a small bowl, season and set aside.

Heat the oil in a large, non-stick frying pan over a medium heat. Fry the onion for 5 minutes until starting to soften. Tip in the garlic, chilli and cumin and continue to fry for 2 minutes, or until fragrant. Stir in the borlotti beans and 50ml (1¾fl oz) of water. Stir for a few minutes, breaking two-thirds of the beans up with the back of a wooden spoon – they should be mostly broken down with a few remaining whole. Fold in the black beans and heat through, then remove from the heat.

Heat a drizzle of oil in another large, non-stick frying pan over a medium heat. Add a tortilla and move around to coat in the oil. Top with one-quarter of the bean mixture and one-quarter of the cheese. Sandwich with a second tortilla, brushing a little oil on its surface. Cook for 4–5 minutes, carefully turning halfway through cooking until golden brown and the cheese is melting. Repeat with the remaining tortillas, beans and cheese.

Slide from the pan onto a board and cut into wedges. Serve with the pico de gallo, soured cream and hot sauce.

KIMCHI-SRIRACHA MAYO &
SESAME TOFU

This posh sandwich is all about texture: crunchy sesame
crust and silky tofu are a match made in heaven in a soft,
buttery brioche roll. The kimchi-sriracha mayo adds an
umami hit you won't be able to resist.

SERVES 2

TAKES 30 minutes

280g (10oz) block extra-firm tofu
2½ tbsp cornflour (cornstarch)
salt and black pepper
1 large egg
7 tbsp mixed black and white
    sesame seeds
3 tbsp light olive oil
½ cucumber, halved lengthways
    and seeds removed
2 spring onions (scallions),
    shredded
1 tsp sesame oil
1 tsp rice vinegar
For the kimchi-Sriracha mayo
2 tbsp shop-bought kimchi,
    shredded
2 tbsp Sriracha chilli sauce
1 tbsp good-quality mayonnaise
1 tbsp clear honey

2 brioche rolls

Cut the tofu into six thick slices. Wrap in kitchen
paper, place a clean board over the top and leave
to stand for 10 minutes.

Meanwhile, put the cornflour on a plate and season.
Beat the egg in a shallow bowl and tip 5 tablespoons
of the sesame seeds onto another plate. Unwrap
the tofu, dust with the seasoned cornflour, then
dip into the egg, shaking off any excess. Plunge into
the sesame seeds and turn until coated in seeds.
Set aside.

Heat the vegetable oil in a large, non-stick frying
pan over a medium–high heat. Fry the tofu for
4–5 minutes, carefully turning halfway through,
until the seeds are crunchy and it is hot through.
Remove from the pan and season.

Thinly slice the cucumber into half-moons and mix
with the spring onions, sesame oil and rice vinegar.

Mix the kimchi, Sriracha, mayo and honey together
in a bowl. Split the brioche rolls and spread with
the sauce. Top with a couple of slices of tofu,
then pile with the cucumber and spring onions.
Sandwich with the tops of the rolls and serve.

GARLIC & TAHINI WITH
★
FALAFEL

Making falafels from scratch requires a little effort, but once you taste these fresh crunchy morsels you'll be glad you didn't plump for their shop-bought counterparts. These go really well with the Classic hummus on page 106.

SERVES 4

TAKES 1 hour, plus overnight soaking

300g (10½oz) dried chickpeas
½ tsp bicarbonate of soda
3 garlic cloves, roughly chopped
1 onion, roughly chopped
1 mild red chilli, roughly chopped
1 tbsp ground cumin
1 tbsp ground coriander
1 tsp sumac, plus extra to serve
handful parsley, chopped
5 tbsp plain (all-purpose) flour
salt and black pepper
150ml (5fl oz) light olive oil
For the garlic tahini sauce
6 tbsp natural yogurt
4 tbsp mayonnaise
juice 1 lemon
1 large garlic clove, crushed
4 tbsp tahini

4 fluffy white flatbreads
crisp chopped salad
pickled chillies and turnips,
   to serve

Put the chickpeas in a large bowl, cover with cold water and leave to soak overnight.

The next day, make the garlic tahini sauce. Mix all the ingredients together, cover and chill.

Drain the chickpeas and dry thoroughly on kitchen paper. Tip into a food processor with the bicarbonate of soda and pulse a couple of times to roughly chop. Add the garlic, onion, chilli, spices and parsley, and pulse to a coarse purée. Add the flour, season and mix well. Divide the mixture into 20 equal portions. Using damp hands, shape the mixture into little patties and place onto a baking sheet. Chill for 10 minutes.

Heat a large, non-stick frying pan over a medium heat. Add about one-third of the oil, then cook the falafels in batches for 6–7 minutes, turning halfway through, until golden and crisp. Drain on kitchen paper, then transfer to a warm oven while you fry the remaining falafels in the rest of the oil.

Serve five falafels per person on a flatbread, spoon over some of the garlic tahini sauce and some chopped salad. Eat immediately with pickled chillies and turnips on the side.

INDIAN-STYLE

★

SPICY POTATOES

This sandwich is perfect any time of day or night when
you are super hungry and only double carbs will do.
Soft white rolls are a must here if you want the ultimate
comforting experience from a sandwich.

 SERVES 4

TAKES 30 minutes

3 medium potatoes
2 tsp turmeric
75g (2½oz) softened butter
2 onions, finely sliced
2 tsp cumin seeds
2 tsp mustard seeds
2 garlic cloves, finely chopped
2 green chillies, finely chopped
2.5-cm (1-in) piece ginger, peeled
  and finely chopped
4 medium tomatoes, deseeded and
  finely chopped
large handful coriander (cilantro),
  roughly chopped
salt and black pepper
8 small or 4 large soft white rolls
2 tbsp light olive oil
1 lime, cut into wedges
mango chutney and hot sauce,
  to serve (optional)

Peel the potatoes and cut into 2-cm (¾-in) dice. Put
the potatoes in a pan of salted water and add half
the turmeric. Bring to the boil, partially cover and
cook for 8 minutes, or until tender. Drain, reserving
about 1 cup of water. Return the potatoes to the
pan and allow to steam-dry for a few minutes.

Meanwhile, heat half the butter in a large frying pan
over a medium heat. Add the onions, cumin and
mustard seeds, and cook for 5 minutes, until the
onions begin to soften and the spices are aromatic.
Add the remaining turmeric, the garlic, chillies and
ginger and cook for 2 minutes.

Tip the potatoes into the pan with 1–2 tablespoons
of the potato cooking water. Stir, breaking up the
potatoes gently with the back of a spoon – you
might have to add all the water to get a good
texture. Gently fold through the tomatoes and
most of the coriander. Season and heat through.

Split the rolls and spread with the remaining butter.
Flash under a hot grill until the butter is melted and
the rolls are lightly golden. Fill each roll generously
with potato mixture and sprinkle with the reserved
coriander. Serve immediately with a lime wedge, a
dollop of mango chutney and hot sauce, if liked.

HONEY-GLAZED

★

PEARS & BLUE CHEESE

This posh open sandwich would not be out of place served as an after-dinner sandwich in place of traditional cheese and crackers. Sweet, salty and thoroughly delicious.

SERVES 4

TAKES 20 minutes

25g (scant 1oz) butter
2 firm ripe pears, cored and each
   cut into 8 wedges
juice ½ lemon
2 tbsp clear honey, plus extra
   to serve
50g (1¾oz) walnuts, toasted and
   roughly chopped
4 slices walnut bread or your
   favourite nutty brown bread
150g (5½oz) blue cheese

Heat the butter in a large, non-stick frying pan over a medium heat. Once bubbling, fry the pear wedges for 5 minutes, turning frequently until they start to take on some colour. Squeeze in the lemon juice and drizzle over the honey. Turn up the heat, throw in the walnut pieces and gently shake the pan until the pears are sticky and tender and the nuts caramelised. Remove from the heat.

Lightly toast the bread on both sides. Remove from the grill, spoon over the pears and any pan juices, dot over the blue cheese and spoon the walnuts over the top. Serve immediately.

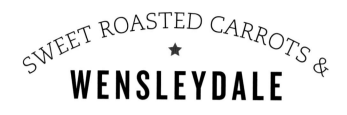

SWEET ROASTED CARROTS &
★
WENSLEYDALE

If you can't find Wensleydale cheese, try a sharp sheep's cheese, or even an aged feta. You want something sharp and salty to stand up to the intense sweetness of the roasted carrots.

SERVES 4

TAKES 1 hour

800g (1lb 12oz) carrots
2 tbsp olive oil
5 sprigs thyme, leaves picked
salt and black pepper
juice and zest 1 orange
2 tbsp clear honey
1 tsp chilli flakes
4 spring onions (scallions),
    finely chopped
150g (5½oz) Wensleydale cheese,
    grated
1 baguette, to serve

Preheat the oven to 190°C/375°F fan/gas 5.

Scrub the carrots and pat dry. Halve any large carrots lengthways, then tip into a roasting tin and toss with the oil and thyme leaves. Season and roast for 45 minutes, stirring halfway through, until golden and tender. Five minutes before the end of cooking, stir in the orange juice and zest, honey and chilli flakes.

Add the spring onions to a bowl with the cheese and stir to combine. Split the baguette in half lengthways, keeping the loaf attached at one side. Spoon the warm carrots and any of their sticky juices over one half. Sprinkle over the cheese and spring onion mixture. Close the baguette, wrap in foil and transfer to a warm oven for 5 minutes. Cut into thick slices and serve.

WHIPPED GOAT'S CHEESE &
★
CAPONATA

Sweet and sour caponata goes so well with everything.
Don't be surprised if you find yourself adding a spoonful
to every sandwich you make, from grilled cheese
to classic burgers.

SERVES 6

TAKES 45 minutes,
plus cooling

4 tbsp olive oil
1 large aubergine (eggplant),
  cut into cubes
1 large onion, finely chopped
3 celery sticks, finely chopped
4 garlic cloves, finely chopped
3 roasted red (bell) peppers from a
  jar, drained and finely chopped
400g (14oz) can chopped tomatoes
3 tbsp red wine vinegar
2 tbsp caster (superfine) sugar
50g (1¾oz) pitted black olives,
  roughly chopped
3 tbsp small capers, drained
2 tbsp sultanas or raisins
salt and black pepper
For the whipped goat's cheese
240g (9oz) soft goat's cheese
5 tbsp Greek yogurt
½ garlic clove, crushed
2 tbsp finely chopped chives

800g (1lb 12oz) focaccia

Heat 3 tablespoons of the oil in a large, non-stick frying pan over a medium–high heat. Cook the aubergine for 8 minutes, stirring frequently, until starting to soften and turn golden. Add the remaining oil and the onion and celery, and fry for 8 minutes, until almost soft and coloured. Add the garlic and cook for a further 2 minutes. Tip the red peppers and tomatoes into the pan and give everything a stir. Bring to the boil, then add the vinegar and sugar. Reduce the heat and cook for 15 minutes, stirring frequently.

Add the olives to the pan with the capers, sultanas and plenty of seasoning. Cook for a further 5 minutes. Remove the pan from the heat and allow to cool. Once cool, taste again and add a little more sugar and/or vinegar to suit your taste.

To make the whipped goat's cheese, put the cheese, yogurt and garlic in a bowl and beat with a wooden spoon until smooth. Stir in most of the chives, reserving a few for later.

Slice the focaccia and warm in a hot oven for a few minutes. Spread with whipped goat's cheese and generously spoon the caponata over the top. Serve immediately, scattered with remaining chives.

Vegetarian Sandwiches

CLASSIC

★

AFTERNOON TEA

The best afternoon tea includes a selection of delicate sandwiches and a delicious slice of cake. Assemble these sandwiches before your guests arrive and have something sweet to bring to the table for the perfect afternoon feast.

EGG & CRESS ROLLS

6 medium eggs
3 tbsp good-quality mayonnaise
1 tsp Dijon mustard
salt and black pepper
12 small bread rolls
cress, to serve

Cook the eggs in a pan of boiling water for 8 minutes. Drain and cool under cold water. Peel and mash with the mayonnaise, mustard and plenty of seasoning. Slice the rolls in half and spread with the egg mayonnaise, sprinkle with cress and sandwich with the lid. Serve immediately.

CUCUMBER FINGER SANDWICHES

8 slices white bread
100g (3½oz) soft cheese
salt and black pepper
½ cucumber

Lay the bread on a board. Season the cheese and beat gently with a spoon to soften, then spread over the bread.

Peel the cucumber so you have alternating stripes of peel and exposed cucumber. Thinly slice. Lay the cucumber slices on top of four slices of bread, then sandwich with the remaining bread. Trim off the crusts and cut each square into three equal-sized fingers. Serve immediately.

🍴 SERVES 6

⏰ TAKES 30 minutes

Pictured with Coronation Chicken Sandwiches (recipe page 61)

SWEET

★

SANDWICHES

CHOUX

★

PASTRY

You can really freestyle with these choux sandwiches. If you don't have a piping bag, just use a couple of teaspoons to dollop the mixture onto the baking sheets, or use a sandwich bag with a corner snipped off.

MAKES 8

TAKES 1 hour, plus cooling

85g (3oz) unsalted butter
140g (5oz) plain (all-purpose)
   flour, sieved
3 medium eggs

Preheat the oven to 200°C/400°F/gas 6. Line two baking sheets with baking parchment.

Dice the butter and put it into a medium saucepan with 225ml (8fl oz) of water. Heat gently until melted, then increase the heat and bring to the boil. Remove the pan from the heat, add the flour and beat the mixture with a wooden spoon until you get a smooth shiny dough that leaves the sides of the pan. Tip into a mixing bowl and allow to cool for 5 minutes.

Lightly whisk the eggs and gradually add them to the dough. Continue to beat until you have a smooth thick dough that falls reluctantly from the spoon. Scrape into a piping bag fitted with a 1.5-cm (½-in) star nozzle and follow the piping instructions for your choux of choice (rings, balls or fingers).

Bake for 20–25 minutes until golden and crisp. Remove from the oven and carefully split in half through the centre. Place cut-side up in pairs on the baking sheets and return to the oven for 5 minutes to dry out and crisp up. Remove from the oven, transfer to a wire rack and allow to cool completely.

COFFEE & WALNUT ★ CHOUX RINGS

Much better than a doughnut – this choux sandwich is the perfect accompaniment to a steaming cup of coffee and a good book.

 MAKES 8

TAKES 1 hour

1 quantity Choux Pastry
(opposite)

For the filling
1 tsp instant coffee powder
600ml (1 pint) double (heavy)
  cream
2 tbsp icing (confectioners') sugar
1 tsp vanilla extract
75g (2½oz) roasted walnuts
For the topping
1 tsp instant coffee powder
150g (5½oz) icing (confectioners')
  sugar
1 tsp vanilla extract

Draw four circles on each sheet of baking parchment using an 8–9-cm (3½-in) round cutter or a glass. Pipe the choux into a ring and smooth any peaks in the pastry with a wet finger. Follow the baking instructions opposite.

To make the filling, dissolve the instant coffee powder in 1 teaspoon of warm water. Put the cream, icing sugar and vanilla in a bowl, add the coffee and whip to soft peaks. Finely chop the roasted walnuts and gently fold through the whipped cream, reserving a few for decoration. Pile the cream into a piping bag fitted with a 1-cm (⅜-in) plain nozzle and pipe one half of the rings. Sandwich with the top halves.

To make the topping, dissolve the coffee in 2 tablespoons of warm water. Sieve the icing sugar into a large bowl and add the vanilla and enough of the coffee liquid to make a thick, smooth, spreadable icing. Spread generously over the tops of the rings, sprinkle with the reserved chopped walnuts and chill until required.

Pictured on page 145 (bottom)

ROSE CREAM
★
CHOUX BUNS

Dainty and delicious, these choux buns are a showstopper at any tea party. Pull out all the stops and sprinkle with edible rose petals for an extra special finish.

MAKES 24

TAKES 1 hour

1 quantity Choux Pastry
(see page 146)

For the filling
600ml (1 pint) double
(heavy) cream
2 tbsp icing (confectioners') sugar
1 tbsp rose water

For the topping
150g (5½oz) icing
(confectioners') sugar
1 tsp rose water
1 tsp vanilla extract
1–2 drops pink food colouring
(optional)
handful edible dried rose petals

Dollop 12 balls of choux on each sheet of baking parchment using a couple of teaspoons. Smooth any peaks in the pastry with a wet finger. Follow the baking instructions on page 146.

To make the filling. Put the cream, icing sugar and rose water in a bowl and whip to soft peaks. Pile the cream into a piping bag fitted with a 1-cm (⅜-in) plain nozzle, or use a couple of teaspoons to cover one half of the buns. Sandwich with the top half and set aside.

To make the topping, sieve the icing sugar into a large bowl and add the rose water, vanilla and a drop of water to make a smooth, spreadable icing. Stir in the pink food colouring (if using) until you have the desired shade of pink. Spread generously over the buns and sprinkle with the rose petals. Chill until ready to serve.

Pictured on page 144 (bottom)

MATCHA & BLACK SESAME
★
CHOUX ECLAIRS

These choux sandwiches are the perfect treat.
An alternative take on the classic eclair but no less
yummy – fusion at its best.

 MAKES 8

TAKES 1 hour

1 quantity Choux Pastry
   (see page 146)

For the filling
1 tsp matcha green tea powder
600ml (1 pint) double
   (heavy) cream
2 tbsp icing (confectioners') sugar
1 tsp vanilla extract
1–2 drops green food colouring
   (optional)
For the topping
½ tsp matcha green tea powder
150g (5½oz) icing
   (confectioners') sugar
1 tsp vanilla extract
1 tbsp black sesame seeds

Pipe four thick 10-cm (4-in) long choux cylinders on each sheet of baking parchment. Smooth any peaks in the pastry with a wet finger. Follow the baking instructions on page 146.

To make the filling, dissolve the matcha powder in 1 teaspoon of warm water. Put the cream, icing sugar and vanilla in a bowl, then add the matcha and green food colouring (if using) and whip to soft peaks. Pile the cream into a piping bag fitted with a 1-cm (⅜-in) plain nozzle, or use a couple of teaspoons to cover one half of each eclair. Sandwich with the top halves and set aside.

To make the topping, dissolve the matcha in 2 teaspoons of warm water. Sieve the icing sugar into a large bowl and add the vanilla and enough of the matcha liquid to make a thick, smooth spreadable icing. Spread generously over the eclairs, sprinkle with the sesame seeds and chill until required.

Pictured on page 144 (top)

THE SHOWSTOPPER
★
VICTORIA SPONGE

Since we're being posh, the top of this classic British sponge
sandwich has been adorned with luscious chocolate-
dipped strawberries. Though not essential, they
do make it look a cut above the rest.

🍴 SERVES 6

⏰ TAKES 45 minutes, plus
cooling

225g (8oz) very soft unsalted
butter, plus extra for greasing
225g (8oz) caster (superfine) sugar
4 large eggs
225g (8oz) self-raising flour
1 tsp baking powder (soda)
**For the chocolate-dipped
strawberries**
75g (2½oz) dark chocolate,
roughly chopped
50g (1¾oz) white chocolate,
roughly chopped
12 strawberries, washed
and hulled
For the filling
300ml (½ pint) double heavy
cream
1 tbsp caster (superfine) sugar
4 tbsp good-quality
strawberry jam

Preheat the oven to 180°C/350°F/gas 4. Grease
and line the base of two 20-cm (8-in) round cake
tins with baking parchment. In a large bowl beat
together all the sponge ingredients until pale and
smooth. Divide the batter equally between the
tins and bake for 20–25 minutes, until risen and
golden. Allow to cool in the tins for 5 minutes,
then transfer to a wire rack.

Line a baking sheet with baking parchment and set
aside. Put the dark and white chocolate into two
separate heatproof bowls. Melt the chocolate in
20-second bursts in the microwave (or over a pan of
simmering water). Dip the strawberries into the dark
chocolate then lay on the baking sheet and chill for
a few minutes. When cool, drizzle with the white
chocolate. Chill until ready to use.

To make the filling, whisk the cream and sugar
together until just spreadable. Spread the jam
over one of the cooled sponges, then dollop over
the cream, saving a little for the top of the cake.
Sandwich the cakes together then spread the
reserved cream over the top. Pop the chocolate-
dipped strawberries on the cream and drizzle over
any leftover melted chocolate.

CHOCOLATE-CHIP COOKIES &
★
ICE CREAM

How to make chewy chocolate chip cookies even better:
sandwich them together with ice cream. Go uber-
chocolatey and use good-quality chocolate ice cream,
or go with a classic vanilla.

SERVES 8

TAKES 25 minutes, plus
chilling and cooling

125g (4½oz) unsalted butter
100g (3½oz) caster (superfine)
  sugar
150g (5½oz) soft light brown sugar
1 large egg
1 tsp vanilla extract
½ tsp salt
225g (8oz) plain (all-purpose) flour
½ tsp bicarbonate of soda
100g (3½oz) dark chocolate chips
50g (1¾oz) milk chocolate chips
good-quality ice cream

Preheat the oven to 180°C/350°F/gas 4. Line two
baking sheets with parchment and set aside.

Melt the butter in a small pan or in the microwave,
then transfer to a large mixing bowl. Add both
types of sugar, the egg, vanilla and salt, and stir
until the mixture is fully combined and smooth.
Tip in the flour and bicarbonate of soda, gently
folding into the wet ingredients and being careful
not to overmix, then stir in the chocolate chips.

Use a couple of dessertspoons to scoop the
mixture onto the prepared trays; you should get
16 cookies. Leave plenty of room for the cookies
to spread during cooking.

Bake for 12–15 minutes until the edges are light
golden. Leave to cool and set on the tray for
10 minutes, then transfer to a wire rack and allow
to cool completely.

Sandwich two cookies together with a scoop
of your favourite ice cream. Eat immediately.

SALTED CARAMEL & ICE CREAM
★
WAFFLES

When a dessert smells and tastes this good it is totally
acceptable to cheat. The trick is to warm the waffles so
they release their sweet, buttery fragrance into the kitchen
– the most delicious shortcut around.

SERVES 2

TAKES 15 minutes

25g (scant 1oz) pecans
knob very soft unsalted butter
pinch salt
4 Belgian butter waffles
2 scoops good-quality vanilla
  ice cream
2 tbsp good-quality salted
  caramel sauce

Preheat the oven to 180°C/350°F/gas 4.

Put the pecans on a large tray, dot over the
butter and sprinkle with a pinch of salt. Bake for
5 minutes, then give the nuts a shake and push to
one side. Lay the waffles on the tray and return
to the oven for 5 more minutes. The nuts should
be fragrant and the waffles just warm. Remove
from the oven.

Put a waffle onto each serving plate and top with a
scoop of ice cream. Drizzle with the caramel sauce,
then roughly crush the nuts with your hands and
sprinkle over the top. Sandwich with the remaining
waffles and serve immediately.

TOASTED CHOCOLATE &
★
OLIVE OIL

Chocolate and olive oil are an unlikely match made in heaven. Add to this mix some good chewy white bread and you will feel like you're eating something far more sinful than you actually are.

SERVES 2

TAKES 10 minutes

4 slices white crusty bread
75g (2½oz) dark chocolate,
   roughly chopped
pinch chilli flakes (optional)
sea salt flakes, for sprinkling
1–2 tbsp olive oil

Divide the chocolate between two slices of bread, then sprinkle with the chilli flakes (if using) and a pinch of salt. Sandwich with the remaining slices of bread.

Heat a large frying pan over a medium–high heat. Brush the top of the sandwiches generously with olive oil. Cook the sandwiches oil-side down for 2 minutes, or until golden. Flip, brush the other side with oil, and cook for a further 2 minutes. The bread should be golden and crisp and the chocolate melted. Serve immediately.

MIXED BERRY

★

CREAM PUFF

If you have people coming round this makes a show-off pud that really couldn't be simpler to put together. Your guests will think you have been to the pâtisserie when they taste these sweet morsels.

SERVES 6

TAKES 30 minutes, plus cooling

320-g (11-oz) packet ready-rolled puff pastry
1 medium egg, lightly beaten
150g (5½oz) frozen summer berries, defrosted
250ml (8¾fl oz) double (heavy) cream
1 tsp vanilla extract or vanilla bean paste
150g (5½oz) icing (confectioners') sugar, plus 1 tbsp

Preheat the oven to 200°C/400°F/gas 6 and line a baking sheet with parchment. Unroll the pastry and lay on the prepared sheet. Cut into 12 equal rectangles and prick six of the rectangles all over with a fork, leaving the remaining six untouched. Brush the surface of the pastry with beaten egg.

Bake for 18–20 minutes, gently flattening the pastry with a spatula halfway through, until puffed and golden. Allow to cool completely on the tray.

Put the berries into a sieve set over a bowl to collect all the juices. Lightly whip the cream with the vanilla extract and 1 tablespoon of icing sugar.

Sieve the remaining icing sugar into a large bowl and add 1 tablespoon of the collected berry juices. Beat with a wooden spoon until smooth – you want an icing with a thick but drizzly consistency; you may need to add a drop more juice.

To assemble the sandwiches, lay the six pricked pastry rectangles on a serving plate, gently pressing down the pastry to flatten it. Ripple the berries into the whipped cream and spoon onto the pastry bases. Sandwich with the remaining pastry and spread with the berry icing. Serve immediately.

MISO PEANUT BUTTER &
★
RASPBERRY

Stirring a spoon of miso into your favourite nut butter is a
game changer and elevates the humble PB&J sandwich
into a grown-up umami fest.

 SERVES 1

TAKES 5 minutes

2 slices good bread (I used
  sourdough)
2 tbsp peanut butter, or your
  favourite nut butter
2 tsp white miso paste
1 tbsp raspberry jam
handful raspberries

Heat the grill to high and lightly toast the bread on
both sides.

Beat the peanut butter and miso paste together
until combined, then spread generously over one
slice of toast.

Spread the raspberry jam over the other slice of
toast and dot the raspberries all over, squashing
them lightly with your finger. Sandwich together,
cut in half and enjoy.

RHUBARB & CUSTARD
★
DOUGHNUTS

Mouth-puckeringly sharp rhubarb and cold silky custard
are old friends and complement each other so well.
If, however, you like something a little sweeter, go for
chopped strawberries or sliced ripe peaches.

SERVES 5

TAKES 20 minutes

400g (14oz) rhubarb
peeled zest 1 orange, plus
    juice ½ orange
75g (2½oz) caster (superfine) sugar,
    plus extra for dusting
5 shop-bought plain or custard
    doughnuts
5 tbsp ready-made custard

Preheat the oven to 200°C/400°F/gas 6.

Trim the rhubarb to remove any gnarly bits, then
cut into 4-cm (1½-in) long pieces. Place in an
ovenproof baking dish with the orange zest, orange
juice and sugar, and toss to combine. Cover with
foil and cook for 15 minutes. Remove the foil,
gently shake the dish, cover again and return to
the oven for 5 minutes. The rhubarb should be just
tender when poked and the juices syrupy. Remove
from the oven and allow to cool completely.

To assemble the sandwiches, cut the doughnuts in
half through the centre, being careful not to lose
any of the custard filling. Add a generous dollop
of fresh custard to the bottom half (whether
using plain or custard doughnuts), then pile on
the rhubarb. Sandwich with the top half of the
doughnut and serve immediately with some of
the syrupy juices spooned over and a dusting
of caster sugar.

MASCARPONE & CHERRY JAM
★
BRIOCHE

These sandwiches are prefect as a sweet offering after a
savoury brunch. Bring all the components to the table
with the fillings and some fresh fruit and let your
guests build their own sandwiches.

 SERVES 8

TAKES 10 minutes

8 chocolate chip brioche rolls
250g (9oz) mascarpone cheese
1 tsp vanilla extract
1 tbsp icing (confectioners') sugar
1–2 tbsp milk
jar good-quality cherry jam

Preheat the oven to 180°C/350°F/gas 4. Heat the
brioche rolls for 5 minutes.

Meanwhile, tip the mascarpone into a mixing bowl
and stir in the vanilla, icing sugar and enough milk
to loosen the mascarpone so that it is spreadable.

Split the brioche rolls in half. Spread the bottom
half with mascarpone, spoon over some cherry
jam and sandwich with the remaining half. Serve
immediately.

BANANA, BACON & BLUEBERRY ★ FRENCH TOAST

This hot, crisp-on-the-outside, gooey-in-the-middle
sandwich has it all. It's perfect for breakfast but also
works well as a (very) indulgent dinner.

SERVES 2

TAKES 20 minutes

4 rashers smoked, streaky bacon
4 slices crusty white bread
2 tbsp peanut butter
1 ripe banana, peeled and sliced
4 medium eggs
100ml (3½fl oz) milk
1 tsp vanilla extract
1 tsp maple syrup
25g (scant 1oz) butter
drizzle light olive oil
For the blueberry sauce
100g (3½oz) blueberries
2 tbsp maple syrup

Heat a large frying pan over a medium heat. Fry the
bacon for about 5 minutes, until golden and crisp.
Transfer to a tray and keep warm in the oven.

Spread 2 slices of bread with the peanut butter.
Lay the banana slices on top of the peanut butter
and sandwich each with the remaining bread. Crack
the eggs into a large, shallow baking dish. Add
the milk, vanilla and maple syrup and whisk until
combined. Soak the sandwiches in the beaten egg
for 5 minutes, turning them over a few times.

Meanwhile, make the blueberry sauce. Heat the
blueberries and maple syrup in a small saucepan
for 3–5 minutes, until the blueberries start to pop.
Allow to bubble for about 1 minute to reduce the
sauce, keeping some blueberries intact. Set aside.

Heat half the butter and oil in a large frying pan
over a medium heat. Once bubbling, lift the
sandwiches out of the egg mixture, shaking off any
excess. Fry the sandwiches for 2–3 minutes, then
turn over. Drop in the remaining butter and fry until
golden, basting with the butter as you go.

Cut the sandwiches in half and serve topped with
crispy bacon and blueberry sauce spooned over.

SCONES

Nothing beats a freshly baked scone, split and thickly buttered or filled with clotted cream, jam and juicy strawberries. This scone recipe also works stuffed with sliced meats and cheese as an alternative to bread.

 SERVES 6

TAKES 20 minutes, plus cooling

225g (8oz) self-raising flour, plus extra for dusting
1 tsp baking powder (soda)
pinch salt
50g (1¾oz) cold unsalted butter, diced
125ml (4fl oz) milk, plus extra for glazing

strawberry jam
clotted cream
150g (5½oz) strawberries, sliced

Preheat the oven to 200°C/400°F/gas 6. Line a baking sheet with baking parchment and set aside.

Put the flour, baking powder and a pinch of salt into a large mixing bowl. Add the butter and rub it into the flour until the mixture resembles fine breadcrumbs. Stir in the milk and use a butter knife to bring the ingredients together. Knead lightly to form a dough.

Tip the dough out onto a lightly floured work surface. Roll or pat the dough out to about 2.5cm (1in) thick and use a 5-cm (2-in) round cutter to stamp out circles, rerolling any offcuts. Transfer the dough circles to the prepared tray and brush the surface of each scone with a little milk. Bake for 12–15 minutes, or until risen and golden. Remove from the oven, transfer to a wire rack and allow to cool to room temperature.

To serve, split the scones in half, spread with jam and top with a dollop of clotted cream and a couple of strawberry slices. Sandwich with the top half of the scone and eat immediately.

LEMON MERINGUE
★
CHEESECAKE KISSES

These sweet little meringue kisses can be made in advance
and stored in an airtight container for up to one month –
just keep a jar of lemon curd in the fridge for the filling.

  MAKES about 20
sandwiches

TAKES 1 hour 30 minutes,
plus cooling

pink gel food colouring
4 medium egg whites
200g (7oz) caster (superfine) sugar
4 digestive biscuits
25g (scant 1oz) unsalted butter
pinch salt
140g (5oz) full-fat cream cheese
4 tbsp good-quality lemon curd

Line two baking sheets with parchment. Fit a
piping bag with a 1-cm (⅜-in) plain nozzle and use
a paintbrush to paint 4 stripes of food colouring
inside the bag, from the tip to the opening.

Preheat the oven to 120°C/250°F/gas ½. Using an
electric hand whisk, beat the egg whites to stiff
peaks. Gradually add the sugar, beating after each
addition, until completely dissolved. The meringue
should stand in stiff peaks and be very glossy.

Fill the piping bag with meringue and twist the top.
Pipe to make a 2-cm (¾-in) base then quickly pull
the bag up to create a peak. Repeat to make 40
meringue kisses. Bake for 1 hour, until the meringues
are dry to the touch. Remove from the oven and
allow to cool completely on the trays.

Meanwhile, put the biscuits in a small bowl and
bash to fine crumbs with the end of a rolling pin.
Melt the butter and mix with the biscuit crumbs
and a pinch of salt. Set aside at room temperature.

Ripple the cream cheese lemon curd together in a
small bowl. Sandwich two meringues together with
a teaspoon of the lemon curd mixture, sprinkle
with buttery crumbs and serve.

INDEX

★★★

ACKNOWLEDGEMENTS

Thank you so much to Sarah, Gemma, Emily, Corinne and Harriet at Quadrille for inviting me to work on another beautiful book!

Thank you to Faith Mason for the great pictures, Alexander Breeze for the amazing props.

Esther Clark for the fun times, your cooking talent and for helping me with the food styling- thank you so much! Jessica Dennison for your help testing recipes, your attention to detail and your all round brilliance. I am really grateful for you two girls for making everything run so smoothly during the shoot and for doing what you do so well!

Dad, thanks for the sandwich idea, such a shame Scouse buttie didn't make the cut!

Finally, thank you to Curt for your unwavering support, love and encouragement.